Ethnic minorities
in the inner city

Richard Dorsett

First published in Great Britain in 1998 by

The Policy Press
University of Bristol
Rodney Lodge
Grange Road
Bristol BS8 4EA
UK

Tel   +44 (0)117 973 8797
Fax   +44 (0)117 973 7308
E-mail   tpp@bristol.ac.uk
Website http://www.bristol.ac.uk/Publications/TPP

In association with the Joseph Rowntree Foundation

ISBN 1 86134 130 X

Photographs used on the front cover were supplied by kind permission of John Birdsall Photography, Nottingham.

Richard Dorsett was formerly a Research Fellow at the Policy Studies Institute in London.

This report forms part of the Fourth National Survey of Ethnic Minorities series. Other publications in the series are published by the Policy Studies Institute, London. They include the highly acclaimed *Ethnic minorities in Britain: Diversity and disadvantage* (1997); *Ethnic minority families* (1998); *The health of Britain's ethnic minorities* (1997); and *Ethnicity and mental health* (1997). For further information, please contact:

Policy Studies Institute
100 Park Village East
London NW1 3SR
E-mail pubs@psi.org.uk

The **Joseph Rowntree Foundation** has supported this project as part of its programme of research and innovative development projects, which it hopes will be of value to policy makers and practitioners. The facts presented and the views expressed in this report, however, are those of the authors and not necessarily those of the Foundation.

Cover design by Qube Design Associates, Bristol.
Printed in Great Britain by Hobbs the Printers Ltd, Southampton.

Contents

Acknowledgements

The Joseph Rowntree Foundation has supported this project as part of its programme of research and innovative development projects, which it hopes will be of value to policy makers and practitioners.

I am very grateful to Tariq Modood, Ceri Peach, Brian Robson, Keith Kirby and Duncan Maclennan for their comments on an earlier draft. I am particularly grateful to Richard Berthoud who provided invaluable advice and encouragement throughout.

The facts presented and views expressed in this report, however, are those of the author and not necessarily those of the Foundation.

Richard Dorsett
Policy Studies Institute

List of tables and figures

Tables

Figures

Glossary of terms used

The need to distinguish between several closely
related measures forces the use of some
specialised vocabulary which assigns particular
meanings for the purpose of this analysis only.

Density   The proportion of the population who are from an ethnic minority group

Concentration   Difference between ward density and conurbation density

Specialisation   The proportion of the minority population accounted for by a single minority

Deprivation   Deprivation as measured by the Department of the Environment's
                             deprivation index

Relative deprivation   The difference between ward deprivation and conurbation deprivation

Executive summary

A large proportion of Britain's ethnic minority population live in the major cities. Higher deprivation for inner cities coupled with the over-representation of ethnic minority groups in these areas results in a tendency for minorities to live in deprived areas.

Different minority groups have different characteristics and it is not appropriate to treat 'ethnic minorities' as if they were a single group subject to identical influences. They:

- tend to be concentrated in different areas;

- are segregated to differing degrees from the white community;

- differ in the extent to which they live in an area populated largely by people from their own ethnic group.

There are important differences according to the socioeconomic characteristics of households and individuals. This study examines how these characteristics are related to patterns of settlement, while acknowledging the complex interplay of individual choice and constraints.

Data and definitions

The main source of data used in this analysis is the Fourth National Survey of Ethnic Minorities. This is combined with further data from two sources. The 1991 Census of Great Britain is used to derive information on areal ethnic mix. Similarly, to get a measure of area deprivation the Department of the Environment's (DoE's) 1991 deprivation index is used. This index condenses a number of indicators of deprivation into a single measure in order to capture something of the multidimensional nature of

deprivation. Two deprivation sub-indices are also considered; one relating to housing deprivation, the other to economic deprivation. The main analysis is carried out at ward level.

The need to distinguish between several closely related measures forces the use of some specialised vocabulary which assigns particular meanings for the purpose of this analysis only.

Density	The proportion of the population who are from an ethnic minority group
Concentration	Difference between ward density and conurbation density
Specialisation	The proportion of the minority population accounted for by a single minority
Deprivation	Deprivation as measured by the Department of the Environment's deprivation index
Relative deprivation	The difference between ward deprivation and conurbation deprivation

The principal focus is on relative measures – concentration and relative deprivation. The reason for this is that location within a conurbation is likely to be determined by factors different from those governing the conurbation in which an individual resides. Choice of location within a conurbation is linked more closely to current preferences and constraints, whereas the reasons for living in any particular conurbation may be partly historical.

Ethnic minority density

There is evidence of segregation since the ethnic minority population density is much higher in those wards in which ethnic minorities live than it is in those wards in which whites live. The ethnic minority population proportion is higher:

- in cities rather than outside cities;

- in London rather than outside London;

- in inner cities rather than outer cities.

London appears different. Minorities in outer London live in wards with a higher minority density than that of the inner London wards in which minorities live.

Overall, Bangladeshis live in areas with the highest minority density. For other minority ethnic groups, the levels are quite similar with the exception of Chinese, for whom the levels are much lower. There are notable differences between conurbations.

There is clear evidence of minority concentration. Whites in all conurbations live in wards where the density of minority ethnic groups is below the ambient density. The reverse is true for ethnic minorities. Again, Bangladeshis and Pakistanis live in wards with the highest minority concentration.

Specialisation is greatest for Indians/African Asians and Pakistanis. In outer London and the West Midlands they tend to live in wards where their own ethnic group accounts for approximately half of all minority ethnic groups. Caribbeans and Bangladeshis have a high level of specialisation in inner London. Chinese have the lowest level of specialisation.

Deprivation

Overall, London has the highest level of deprivation and the West Midlands has the second highest. London has much higher housing deprivation than the other conurbations.

Whites live in wards with a lower level of deprivation than those in which ethnic minorities live. The only exception to this is in inner London, where the level of ward deprivation for whites and non-whites is broadly similar. Deprivation is much higher for whites in London than in other cities. The same is not true of minorities; the level of deprivation in other inner cities is only slightly below that in inner London itself.

Overall, Bangladeshis live in the most deprived wards, followed by Pakistanis and Caribbeans. Indians live in wards with a slightly higher level of deprivation than those in which African Asians and Chinese live. Whites live in wards with the lowest levels of deprivation.

There is variation between conurbations. In London, Bangladeshis and Caribbeans live in the most deprived wards while Indians and African Asians live in wards less deprived than those in which whites live. The West Midlands has the highest levels of deprivation for Indians, African Asians and Pakistanis.

Across all conurbations, Pakistanis and Bangladeshis are the ethnic groups living in the wards with the highest level of deprivation relative to that of their conurbation. Caribbeans follow some way behind. Indians and Chinese have a lower level of relative deprivation, while whites and African Asians have the lowest level of all.

The effect of individual and household characteristics

Modelling concentration and relative deprivation showed how specific characteristics were associated with ward deprivation and concentration, *after taking account of other factors*:

- In London, whites were predicted to live in wards with a higher level of relative deprivation than Indian and African Asian Hindus with identical characteristics. Pakistanis and Chinese were predicted to live in wards with equal levels of relative deprivation. Bangladeshis and, in particular, Caribbeans are predicted to live in the most deprived wards. Whites and Chinese are likely to live in wards with much lower ethnic minority density than London as a whole. There is a noticeable South Asian effect: Indian and African Asian Hindus,

Pakistanis and Bangladeshis all live in wards with high levels of concentration.

- Those with a lower income were predicted to live in wards with a higher level of relative deprivation. There was a negligible effect on concentration for whites. For the minority ethnic groups, those on lower incomes will tend to live in areas with higher concentration and vice versa.

- Being an owner-occupier is associated with living in an area with lower relative deprivation than other tenure arrangements. It also increases concentration for all ethnic groups, although the effect is only slight for whites.

- Being in a higher social class is associated with living in a ward with lower relative deprivation. Those in the highest social class also live in areas with a lower ethnic minority concentration.

- Being educated to 'A'-level standard or higher does not affect the predicted level of relative deprivation for whites but, for minorities, it is associated with a reduced level of deprivation. Ethnic minorities with qualifications at this level are likely to live in wards with a lower level of concentration. Those who are not fluent in English are more likely to live in areas with a higher ethnic minority concentration.

- Whites in the West Midlands tend to live in wards with much lower levels of relative deprivation than whites in London. The level of ethnic minority concentration for whites is also lower than in London. For most other ethnic groups, particularly African Asian and Indian Hindus, there is a large increase in deprivation associated with living in the West Midlands rather than London. The effect on concentration is more varied. Caribbeans, Pakistanis and Bangladeshis are likely to live in wards with a higher level of concentration in the West Midlands, while the reverse is true for Indian and African Asian Hindus.

- There is a religious dimension with Indians and African Asians who are Muslim living in wards with a higher level of deprivation than Hindus and Sikhs. There is not a consistent pattern when we consider concentration, but for all three religions, the associated level of concentration is higher for Indians than for African Asians. It is mainly Hindus and Sikhs who live in wards of high concentration but low deprivation.

Conclusions and implications

Bangladeshis and Pakistanis stand out as living in wards with the highest levels of relative deprivation and concentration. It is only among Indians and African Asians that high concentration is unmatched by high deprivation: this suggests the existence of relatively well-off communities among these ethnic groups.

The principal evidence of relatively affluent ethnic minority communities relates to South Asians in London, with the exception of Bangladeshis. It is this group and their prevalence in the relatively affluent areas of outer London that breaks the generalisation that concentration is synonymous with deprivation. This suggests that South Asian patterns of settlement are typically non-dispersing and that the existence of South Asian enclaves is, at least in part, the result of choice rather than negatively imposed constraints.

Urban policy must achieve a delicate balance and reflect the fact that both choices and constraints are important in determining residential location. While the deprivation of those areas in which ethnic minorities live is a clear-cut issue deserving of attention, tackling segregation is not so straightforward – many individuals from ethnic minorities will choose to live in areas where their own ethnic group, or other minority groups, are well-represented.

Introduction

A large proportion of Britain's ethnic minority population live in the major cities – London and the main industrial centres. Within these cities, they are often concentrated in the poorest and most run-down areas, the same areas which provide the main focus for regeneration programmes. Such regeneration efforts aim to improve the prospects of all the residents of target areas. However, given their over-representation, it is essential in the formulation or study of urban policy to pay explicit attention to the circumstances, experiences and needs of minority ethnic groups.

In broad terms, we already know where minority groups live. For the first time, direct information on ethnicity was collected in the 1991 Census and this has allowed researchers to examine different aspects of the ethnic minority population in Britain (OPCS, 1996). The Census shows ethnic minorities to account for 5.5% of the population of Great Britain, mainly in England. Their geographic distribution is uneven. For example, they are almost completely absent from Cumbria whereas in the London Borough of Brent 45% of the population belongs to an ethnic minority.

When smaller geographic areas are considered, further evidence of concentration is discovered. In fact, a large proportion of the ethnic minority population is concentrated in a relatively small number of wards. Within these wards, the minority population proportion can reach very high levels. The highest is in Northcote ward in Ealing (over 90%). Spinney Hill ward in Leicester has the second highest proportion, at 83%. Furthermore, if we consider a yet finer level of disaggregation, the Enumeration District (ED), the findings appear even more dramatic. Of particular note is the extent to which

individual ethnic minority groups begin to account for large proportions of the population. For example, Peach (1996) shows that for one ED in Spitalfields, 90% of the population was Bangladeshi.

This concentration of ethnic minority groups is very notable but differs considerably from the concentration of African-Americans in the US. Ghettos are characterised by two properties (Peach, 1996). First, a single ethnic or racial group forms the whole population of the residential district. Second, most members of that group are found in such areas. In US cities, areas of 100% African-American population are commonly found. Duncan and Duncan (1957) showed that by 1950, over half the black population of Chicago was living in areas which were 100% black and that just less than 80% were living in areas which were 90% black. Since that time, African-American segregation has remained very high. While ghettos can be said to exist in the US, therefore, they are not an appropriate model for Britain. The very high representation of a single ethnic minority group within the population of an area is not consistently achieved. Consequently, the second defining characteristic of a ghetto is not satisfied.

Although the levels of segregation in Britain do not match those of the US, there is clearly a concentration of ethnic minorities in the major conurbations, and in certain areas within these conurbations. This has implications for standard of living since it is in the big cities, and in particular the inner cities, where deprivation is at its highest. Robson and Tye (1995), for example, show that the 16 local authority districts with the highest measured deprivation "comprise 10 inner London boroughs and

Greenwich, two Midland districts (Birmingham and Sandwell) and three North West districts (Liverpool, Knowsley and Manchester)". Thus, higher deprivation for inner cities coupled with the over-representation of ethnic minority groups in these areas implies a tendency for minorities to live in deprived areas.

This is indeed the case and has long been recognised as such (Smith, 1989). For example, 45% of minority adults interviewed in the Policy Studies Institute's (PSI's) Fourth National Survey of Ethnic Minorities lived in areas which are 'striving' according to the ACORN classification. Modood et al (1997) considered the housing of ethnic minorities and found that they were more likely than whites to mention environmental problems such as graffiti, vandalism and vermin infestation. They were also more likely to report problems of personal and property crime. This is a reflection of the deprivation of their areas relative to those of whites.

However, the over-representation of ethnic minorities in deprived areas has never been analysed in sufficient detail to reveal clearly what has been happening. All sorts of processes may have been important. For example, it is possible that:

- minorities, having high rates of unemployment and poverty, can only find accommodation in areas of cheap housing, where their neighbours are also likely to be unemployed and/or poor;

- racial discrimination has excluded minorities from prosperous areas, so they have to live in deprived areas;

- minorities tend to live near each other because of chain migration and community commitments. Because as a group they have high rates of unemployment and poverty, the places where they live register as deprived.

Thus, we can see that both choices and constraints may be important in determining residential location. As a positive example, ethnic minorities may prefer to live in areas where their ethnicity is well-represented for reasons of social support, shared cultural and other values and traditions. However, it is possible that their location in certain areas may reflect a constraint rather than a choice. Barriers may exist which hinder easy movement

to new areas. Such barriers may take the form of economic weakness or discrimination from the white community, for example.

It is important to understand the patterns of settlement for ethnic minorities if policy is to accurately reflect the full diversity of multicultural Britain. This is particularly so given the delicate balance which policy must achieve. While the deprivation of those areas in which ethnic minorities live is a clear-cut issue deserving of attention, tackling segregation is not so straightforward. Restrictions (implicit or otherwise) on the extent to which ethnic minorities are able to choose their place of residence can only be regarded as a negative factor. However, policy makers must be sensitive to the fact that many individuals from ethnic minorities will choose to live in areas where their own ethnic group, or other minority groups, are well-represented. The continuance of such local communities may be instrumental to the preservation of ethnic minority identities. However, it is not immediately obvious how to distinguish between choice and constraint in the decision to live in an area of ethnic minority concentration. What may appear to be a self-contained ethnic minority community may, in reality, be a group of marginalised families and individuals forced together by external adversity and reluctant to move from the security of their community due to negative experiences elsewhere. In this case, the segregation of the ethnic minority community creates an isolated group of individuals and runs counter to the aim of integration.

The Fourth Survey examined individuals' preferred ethnic mix in their local area. A high proportion of respondents claimed to have no preference in the matter. This was particularly true of Indians and African Asians, approximately 60% of whom had no stated preference. It was only among whites and Chinese that there was a substantial proportion preferring that fewer than half of local residents come from ethnic minorities. Conversely, a substantial proportion of Caribbeans, Pakistanis and Bangladeshis said they would prefer to live in an area with more than half the population belonging to an ethnic minority. Considering the preferred proportion of the local population belonging to the respondents' own ethnic group revealed an inconsistency; for all except the Bangladeshis, the preferred proportion of own ethnic group in the local area exceeded the stated preferred proportion of ethnic minorities. This is shown in Table 1.1 below.

These are important issues for those involved in urban and social policy. Local authorities need to have an appreciation of where ethnic minorities are and where they will move in the future. Such an understanding will prove invaluable in planning services and community infrastructure to adequately meet the needs of the local population.

It is also important to appreciate the differences between ethnic minority groups. Different groups tend to predominate in different areas. Furthermore, as well as differences between minority groups in the extent to which they are segregated from the white community, there are also differences in the extent to which they live in an area populated largely by people from their own ethnic group. Peach (1996) uses the 1991 Census to show that Bangladeshis have the highest levels of segregation, followed by Pakistanis (see next chapter). Indians have a much lower level of segregation, and Caribbeans lower still. Since different areas tend to be characterised by different levels of deprivation, there are important differences between ethnic minority groups in the extent to which they live in deprived areas.

These differences between minority ethnic groups reflect a range of factors. Originally, migrant groups from different parts of the world tended to have different profiles of skills and experience, leading them to seek employment in different industries (Modood et al, 1997). In addition, within ethnic groups there is substantial variation in socioeconomic characteristics, and these characteristics are significantly related to location. The statement that ethnic minorities tend to live in deprived places is too general and needs to be unpacked.

Objectives

The publication of the Fourth Survey represents a significant advance in our understanding of the economic, social, cultural and other characteristics of ethnic minorities. The aim of this report is to further explore one issue which was touched upon in the Fourth Survey: namely, patterns of ethnic minority settlement. With this in mind, we consider both the tendency for minority ethnic groups to be concentrated within certain areas, and the tendency for them to live in deprived areas. This distinction is important since, as we shall see, ethnic minority concentration is not coterminous with deprivation. While these two characteristics of an area are undoubtedly correlated, there are some important exceptions. These exceptions are of great policy interest.

With regard to deprivation, the focus is on areal deprivation rather than the deprivation of the ethnic groups themselves (which has received considerable attention in the Fourth Survey). This is an important conceptual distinction, although the two aspects of deprivation are

Table 1.1: Preferred ethnic mix in local area (%)

Conurbation				Ethnic group			
	White	Caribbean	Indian	African Asian	Pakistani	Bangladeshi	Chinese
Proportion of ethnic minorities							
No preference	39	42	60	55	38	38	46
Fewer than half	51	16	16	16	16	18	34
More than half	10	41	24	29	46	44	20
Proportion of own ethnic group							
No preference		41	56	50	35	42	42
Fewer than half		12	15	17	13	16	32
More than half		47	29	33	51	42	25

closely related. Since the measure of areal deprivation is based on Census information (see below), the characteristics of individuals and households en masse within an area determine deprivation of that area. However, at the level of the individual it is safe to assume that socioeconomic characteristics vary independently of those of the local area and therefore it is valid to compare household disadvantage with ambient deprivation. Clearly, there will be household variations within areas and it is not possible to infer that a household is deprived simply because of its location within a deprived area. These apparent inconsistencies between areal and household characteristics form a major focus of the analysis to follow (see Massey and Denton, 1993, for the most recent major statement of the importance of the local social ecology to behaviour).

The area in which an individual lives is influenced by a number of factors. In particular, there are likely to be significant variations across ethnic groups: it is not appropriate to treat 'ethnic minorities' as if they were a single group subject to identical influences. The first stage in this analysis will be to analyse the patterns of residence of different minority groups more carefully:

- It is clear that they live in different, though overlapping, areas. While Bangladeshis are highly segregated, people of Chinese origin are widely distributed and cannot be said to be segregated at all when considering ward-level data (Peach, 1996).

- They have very different tenure patterns: Caribbeans and Bangladeshis are commonly found in social housing while Indians, African Asians and Pakistanis tend more to be found in owner-occupation (Jones, 1993; Modood et al, 1997).

- They have experienced different economic trajectories, so that African Asians and Indians are in a similar position to white people, while Pakistanis and Bangladeshis have very high rates of poverty (Modood et al, 1997).

These three factors make it likely that some minority groups are more represented in deprived areas than others, and at different concentrations.

There are also likely to be important differences according to the socioeconomic characteristics of households and individuals. The second stage of the analysis will be to distinguish between individuals within each ethnic minority group. Given a tendency to live near other members of their group and to live in deprived areas, who are the people who do not fit that pattern? To what extent do the characteristics of households and individuals reflect or differ from those of their local ecology? The answers to questions such as these would not only generate a much clearer picture of the minority populations of the areas targeted by regeneration policy, but would provide some clues about the future trends in the patterns of settlement.

Data

The main source of data used in this analysis is the Fourth National Survey of Ethnic Minorities (Modood et al, 1997). This was undertaken in 1994 by the PSI and Social and Community Planning Research (SCPR). It is a nationally representative sample of 5,196 people of Caribbean and Asian origin who were interviewed in detail, together with a comparison sample of 2,867 white people. The survey collects information on education, employment and housing as well as income, health, harassment and ethnic identity. A full set of the survey questionnaires can be found in Smith and Prior (1996).

The Fourth Survey represents an immensely valuable resource for the analysis of ethnic minorities in England and Wales. Whereas the Census was primarily concerned with the 94.5% non-minority population, the Fourth Survey focuses explicitly on the 5.5% minority population. It is thus able to cover topics of particular relevance to ethnic minorities such as cultural identity, religion, dress, linguistic fluency and a range of other characteristics. Since it was carried out at roughly the same time as the Census, there is scope for complementarity between these two data sources.

Indeed, the 1991 Census of Great Britain is used to calculate the density of ethnic minority groups at successive levels of area definition. This information is combined with the Fourth Survey in order to get a measure of the ethnic mix of the area in which a household is situated. Similarly, to get a measure of area deprivation the DoE's 1991 deprivation index (Robson and Tye, 1995) is used. This index condenses a number of indicators of deprivation into a single measure in order to capture something of the multidimensional nature of deprivation. The index is constructed for three levels of spatial disaggregation: district, ward and ED. At ward level, seven indicators, all drawn from the 1991 Census, make up the index. These are:

- total unemployment rate (unemployed economically active persons: total economically active);

- lacking a car (households with no car: total households);

- children in low-income households (number of children in households with no earner or with a single parent in part-time work: total children);

- overcrowding (households living at over one person per room: total households);

- lacking amenities (residents in households lacking the standard amenities of bath/ shower or toilet: total residents in households);

- children in unsuitable accommodation (children living in purpose-built flats or in non-permanent or shared accommodation: total children);

- educational participation (persons aged 17 not in full-time education: total 17-year-olds).

As well as being used to calculate an overall measure of deprivation, individual indicators may be combined to form deprivation sub-indices. The DoE report considers two sub-indices:

housing: comprising children in unsuitable accommodation and households lacking amenities;

economic: comprising the remaining indicators.

Thus, the Fourth Survey is augmented by this area-specific information. It is this composite dataset which forms the basis for the analysis in this report.

Level of analysis

Finally, before presenting the analysis proper, we must choose the size of area which is to provide the basis for the analysis. The DoE deprivation index is calculated at the district, ward and ED level, as already noted. We can therefore derive a conurbation-level measure of deprivation, for example, as the average deprivation of its component districts, wards or EDs. This choice could have a marked effect on the results. For example, Peach (1996) found that people of Chinese origin are not segregated from most groups at the ward level, but are highly segregated at the ED level. This suggests that Chinese are well-distributed across conurbations but in a series of segregated clusters that reveal themselves at finer levels of disaggregation.

In the analysis that follows, it is the ward rather than the district or ED which will be the basic unit in the analysis, and conurbation-level measures are constructed as the average values across wards. The choice of ward is appropriate for a number of reasons. First, the district is typically too large and diverse an area to provide a useful insight into the extent to which the minority ethnic population is concentrated. Within many districts, there are likely to be areas with populations of greatly differing ethnic composition. Similarly, within many districts there will be areas with high levels of deprivation as well as areas with low levels. This suggests a smaller level of geographic disaggregation would be appropriate. The next smallest area on which information is available is the ward. This is likely to be more homogeneous in the ethnicity of its population and in its level of deprivation, and is therefore to be preferred. Thus, in addition to capturing the variation between districts, focusing on wards also captures the variation within districts. It also has some intuitive appeal since wards are of such a size as to broadly coincide with the concept of a neighbourhood or community.

It would be possible to produce an even finer grain analysis by focusing on the ED. This, however, presents practical problems since the ED was not recorded for the sample of white households in the Fourth Survey. Regardless of this, the number of households comprising each ED may be too small to be felt to represent a community. Hence, consideration of ward level information appears to offer a useful compromise between the broad-brush district information and the very specific ED information.

Outline of the report

In the next chapter we consider the issue of ethnic minority density of wards. This is followed in Chapter 4 by an analysis of the distinct (though perhaps related) issue of wards deprivation. In Chapter 5 we consider how individuals with different personal characteristics tend to live in wards with different levels of density and deprivation. This is examined more formally in the context of a statistical model in Chapter 5. Chapter 6 discusses the policy implications and concludes.

Ethnic minority density

We have stated that the ethnic minority population is concentrated within urban areas. The extent to which this is the case can be seen by inspecting the data from the 1991 Census. Tables 2.1(a) and 2.1(b) show how the population of ethnic groups (as defined in the Census) is divided between the regions of England. This is presented in the form of both raw numbers and percentages. This same information is summarised in a simplified form in Figure 2.1 below. These pie charts show, for whites and ethnic minorities, the extent to which the population is concentrated within the main conurbations. The results are striking.

While more than half of whites live outside the principal urbanised areas of England, the corresponding percentage for ethnic minorities is only 15%. It is in London and the West Midlands where the contrasts are the most stark. While only 4% of whites live in inner London, 22% of ethnic minorities are found here. Similarly, outer London accounts for only 8% of whites compared with 24% of ethnic minorities. Close to half of all England's ethnic minorities live in London. In the West Midlands the discrepancy is smaller but still notable. A total of 5% of whites and 13% of ethnic minorities live in this area.

Figure 2.1: The over-representation of ethnic minorities in urban areas

Whites

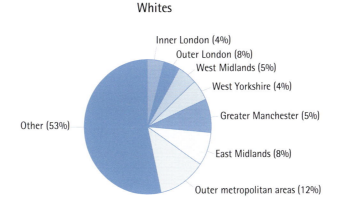

Ethnic minorities

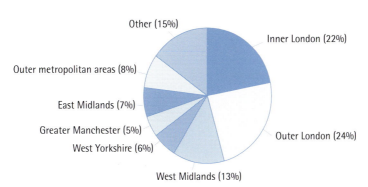

Table 2.1(a): Estimates of ethnic group populations for regions in Great Britain (1,000s)

	White	All minorities	Black Caribbean	Black African	Black other	Indian	Pakistani	Bangladeshi	Chinese	Other Asian	Other other
Inner London	1,949	678	188	114	53	78	31	75	29	48	61
Outer London	3,535	728	116	56	32	283	61	15	29	70	65
West Midlands	2,237	392	76	4	17	148	93	19	6	9	20
West Yorkshire	1,912	173	16	3	7	37	85	6	4	5	11
Greater Manchester	2,414	156	18	6	10	31	52	12	9	5	14
East Midlands	3,837	198	26	4	11	105	19	4	8	7	15
Outer metropolitan area	5,384	242	28	7	12	74	47	11	16	19	28
North West – rest	2,303	73	2	1	3	24	28	3	3	3	6
South Yorkshire	1,264	38	6	1	3	4	14	1	2	1	5
South East – rest	5,006	115	13	6	10	27	10	7	11	10	20
East Anglia	2,037	44	5	2	7	7	6	2	4	4	8
West Midlands – rest	2,584	52	6	1	3	18	11	1	3	3	6
Merseyside	1,422	27	2	3	5	3	1	1	6	1	6
Tyne & Wear	1,109	21	0	1	1	4	4	3	3	2	3
South West	4,653	65	13	3	7	11	4	2	7	4	13
North – rest	1,942	19	1	1	1	4	6	1	2	1	3
Yorkshire/Humberside – rest	1,582	14	1	1	1	2	1	1	2	1	3
England	45,172	3,036	518	214	182	860	472	166	145	194	285

Table 2.1(b): Estimates of ethnic group populations for regions in Great Britain (%)

	White	All minorities	Black Caribbean	Black African	Black other	Indian	Pakistani	Bangladeshi	Chinese	Other Asian	Other other
Inner London	4	22	36	53	29	9	7	45	20	25	22
Outer London	8	24	22	26	18	33	13	9	20	36	23
West Midlands	5	13	15	2	9	17	20	12	4	5	7
West Yorkshire	4	6	3	1	4	4	18	4	3	2	4
Greater Manchester	5	5	4	3	5	4	11	7	6	3	5
East Midlands	8	7	5	2	6	12	4	3	5	4	5
Outer metropolitan area	12	8	5	3	6	9	10	7	11	10	10
North West – rest	5	2	0	1	1	3	6	2	2	1	2
South Yorkshire	3	1	1	1	2	0	3	1	2	1	2
South East – rest	11	4	3	3	5	3	2	4	8	5	7
East Anglia	5	1	1	1	4	1	1	1	3	2	3
West Midlands – rest	6	2	1	1	2	2	2	1	2	1	2
Merseyside	3	1	0	1	3	0	0	0	4	1	2
Tyne & Wear	2	1	0	0	0	1	1	2	2	1	1
South West	10	2	2	1	4	1	1	1	5	2	5
North – rest	4	1	0	0	1	0	1	0	2	1	1
Yorkshire/Humberside – rest	4	0	0	0	1	0	0	1	2	1	1
England	100	100	100	100	100	100	100	100	100	100	100

Table 2.2: Greater London indices of dissimilarity by ethnicity (1991)

	White	Black Caribbean	Black African	Black other	Indian	Pakistani	Bangladeshi	Chinese	Other Asian	Other other	Non-white
White		49	46	41	51	54	65	30	34	29	35
Black Caribbean	54		21	15	56	51	62	42	43	35	29
Black African	56	35		19	56	51	57	34	39	33	27
Black Other	52	32	39		55	51	60	35	39	29	25
Indian	56	62	64	65		33	67	49	38	45	36
Pakistani	66	62	64	65	48		65	51	41	46	36
Bangladeshi	77	74	71	74	78	77		59	60	59	54
Chinese	52	60	57	60	64	70	77		27	23	27
Other Asian	47	54	54	55	50	58	76	53		22	23
Other Other	39	46	47	46	54	61	74	52	43		19
Non-white	40	33	36	37	40	48	67	49	36	31	

Note: ward level above diagonal, ED level below.

Using the Census data, Peach (1996) calculated indices of dissimilarity to show the extent to which segregation exists between ethnic groups. One of his tables, relating to segregation in Greater London, is reproduced as Table 2.2. A high value of the index of dissimilarity indicates a high level of segregation. Thus, the figures show that ethnic minority groups differ in the extent to which they are segregated both from whites and from other ethnic minorities. Bangladeshis are the most segregated ethnic minority group, irrespective of whether we consider ward-level or ED-level information.

For the remainder of this report, the analysis is based on those individuals interviewed in the Fourth Survey. In this section we turn our attention to an explicit consideration of the extent to which ethnic minority groups live in wards where ethnic minorities form a large proportion of the population. We shall refer to this proportion as the ethnic minority 'density'. We are also interested in the extent to which minority groups tend to live in areas where the proportion of the population from the household's particular ethnic group is high.

Both aspects were considered by Modood et al (1997). They found strong evidence of segregation with the average proportion of ethnic minorities being less than one in 20 in those wards where white respondents lived. For Caribbeans and Indians/African Asians, this proportion rose to a quarter, while for Pakistanis and Bangladeshis it was one third. Chinese were found to be the least segregated. This overall pattern was repeated when considering the respondents' own ethnic groups, except that now Indians/African Asians were similar to Pakistanis and Bangladeshis in being the most likely to live in areas where their own ethnic groups were well-represented.

We can examine how ethnic minority density varies for our sample between types of area. The following tables present the average levels of density by ethnic group across the wards within each type of area. In the remainder of this chapter we consider the extent to which these overall patterns vary when considering different types of area.

Minority ethnic density by type of area

In the tables that follow, we consider a number of different groupings of wards in order to explicitly focus on particular aspects of the variations in ethnic minority density. Thus, we consider those wards which are outside cities compared with those which fall within cities. We also consider London compared with other cities. Another grouping allows comparison of the inner city with outer city areas. For each of these groupings, the ethnic minority density is calculated as the average density across the constituent wards. Since different ethnic minority groups tend to be more or less represented in different wards, these levels of density can be separately calculated for each ethnic group. We begin, however, by considering the crude division of the sample into whites and non-whites.

Table 2.3 shows how, across all areas, the minority density is much higher in those wards in which ethnic minorities live than it is in those wards in which whites live. To some extent this is tautologous, but it is revealing to see the robustness of this finding: in those wards in which whites live, only 4% of the population belongs to an ethnic minority, whereas in those wards where ethnic minorities live, a quarter of the population belongs to an ethnic minority. This provides further evidence of segregation. Wards in cities have much higher levels of ethnic minority density than do wards outside cities. This is true for both whites and non-whites, although the overall level remains much higher for non-whites (approximately one third of the population of those city wards resident to non-whites belong to an ethnic minority). The extent to which minorities' own ethnic groups are represented within their wards follows a similar pattern. In cities, the level of representation is much higher than outside cities.

We have already seen in Figure 2.1 the extent to which the ethnic minority population is concentrated in London. Given its importance, Table 2.4 distinguishes between London and elsewhere in presenting minority density for all cities. The striking feature of this table is the difference between London and other cities in the level of ethnic minority density in those wards in which whites live: whereas the density in other cities is only 4%, in London it is 18%. This suggests that segregation is less marked in London than in provincial cities. Conversely, there is little difference between London and other cities for those wards in which minorities live. This is true of both density and the representation of minorities' own ethnic groups.

Table 2.3: Minority ethnic group density of urban versus non-urban areas (%)[1]

| Type of area | Whites | Minorities | |
	Minority density	Minority density	Own ethnic group density
City*	8	32	13
Not city	3	10	5
All types of area	4	26	11

Note: * London, West Midlands, Greater Manchester, South Yorkshire, West Yorkshire, Merseyside and Tyne and Wear conurbations.

[1] For Table 2.3 and the following tables, the 'minority density' entries in each table cell are calculated as the average minority density for the wards in which households within that cell are situated. Similarly, the 'own ethnic group density' entries in each table cell are calculated as the average own ethnic group density for the wards in which households within that cell are situated.

Table 2.4: Minority ethnic group density of London versus other cities (%)

| Type of area | Whites | Minorities | |
	Minority density	Minority density	Own ethnic group density
London	18	34	14
Other cities	4	30	12
All cities	8	32	13

In Table 2.5 the difference between inner and outer cities is highlighted. Overall, minority density is shown to be much higher in inner cities. Again, this distinction is particularly marked for whites. Ethnic minority density in those outer city wards in which whites live is only 5% compared with 12% for the inner city wards. The corresponding levels for ethnic minority wards are more equally matched.

Table 2.5: Minority ethnic group density of inner city versus outer city (%)

| Type of area | Whites | Minorities | |
	Minority density	Minority density	Own ethnic group density
Inner city*	12	35	12
Outer city†	5	30	14
All cities	8	32	13

*Notes: * Inner London, Birmingham, Manchester, Sheffield, Leeds, Liverpool, Newcastle.*
† Outer London, West Midlands, Greater Manchester, South Yorkshire, West Yorkshire, Merseyside, Tyne and Wear.

These tables indicate that a high ethnic minority density is principally an urban characteristic. It is more typical of London than other cities and of inner city areas rather than surrounding metropolitan areas. Furthermore, the relativities of white and minority areas suggest that segregation is lower in London than in other cities and that it is also lower in inner city areas.

However, Table 2.6 reveals further subtleties by distinguishing between inner and outer London and the inner and outer areas of other cities. Our findings so far suggest that the level of segregation as indicated by the ethnic minority density of white compared to non-white areas should be lowest in inner London. This is shown to be the case: it is here that the levels of density for whites and minorities are the closest. We can also see that the higher density associated with living in the inner city is not geographically invariant. That is to say, whites in cities other than London live in wards with similar levels of ethnic minority density regardless of whether they are in the inner or outer city. Conversely, minorities in outer London live in wards with slightly higher levels of density than those in inner London, whereas elsewhere it is the inner city which is characterised by higher levels for minorities. Taken together, these findings appear to suggest that there is something qualitatively different about the inner and outer city divide in London compared with other cities.

Table 2.6: Minority ethnic group density by type of city (%)

| Type of city | Whites | Minorities | |
	Minority density	Minority density	Own ethnic group density
Inner London	21	32	12
Outer London	12	35	15
Other inner city	4	40	12
Other outer city	3	22	11
All cities	32	8	13

Table 2.7 shows the ethnic minority density for the five conurbations which are the main areas of ethnic minority settlement and form the primary focus of this study. If we consider the main conurbations for minority ethnic groups, we see that minorities in London, the West Midlands and West Yorkshire all live in wards where the level of ethnic minority density is about one third. Again, those regions with a high minority density are also those with a high representation of minorities from the households' own ethnic group. As we have already seen, it is only in London that the difference between whites and ethnic minorities in terms of minority density is narrowed at all. However, even here ethnic minorities live in wards with a density twice that of the wards in which whites live.

Table 2.7: Minority ethnic group density by conurbation (%)

| Conurbation | Whites | Minorities | |
	Minority density	Minority density	Own ethnic group density
London	18	34	14
Greater Manchester	6	16	8
South Yorkshire	1	19	6
West Midlands	8	33	12
West Yorkshire	3	33	15
Elsewhere	3	10	5
All areas	4	26	11

Table 2.8: Minority ethnic group density by conurbation (%)

Conurbation	Ethnic group						
	White	Caribbean	Indian	African Asian	Pakistani	Bangladeshi	Chinese
London	18	32	39	35	36	39	21
Greater Manchester	6	-	-	-	20	34	-
South Yorkshire	-	-	-	-	15	-	-
West Midlands	8	39	25	32	41	43	-
West Yorkshire	3	27	-	-	43	-	-
Elsewhere	3	7	11	14	16	16	4
All areas	4	26	25	26	28	34	13

The clear finding from these tables is that minority ethnic groups do tend to be segregated from the main areas of white residence, both between conurbations and within conurbations. On the other hand, it can be seen that levels of segregation are nowhere near those seen in the 'ghettos' identified in the US.

Table 2.8 considers density by conurbation for all ethnic groups. We see that, overall, Bangladeshis live in areas with the highest minority density. For other minority ethnic groups, the levels are quite similar with the exception of Chinese. There are notable differences between conurbations. Indians and Bangladeshis in London live in wards where the minority density is highest. In fact, Indians and African Asians live predominantly in outer London while Bangladeshis live mainly in inner London. The levels for Chinese in London are only slightly higher than those for whites. Outside London, the differences between whites and other ethnic groups are greater. Bangladeshis and Pakistanis in the West Midlands live in wards with a very high minority density, as do Caribbeans. The highest density for Pakistanis is among those living in West Yorkshire. The difference in density between the wards in West Yorkshire in which Pakistanis live and those in which whites live represents the greatest difference between any two ethnic groups in any of the conurbations.

When considering the representation of minorities' own ethnic groups, it is interesting to note the degree to which different minorities have established themselves in different areas. This is shown in Table 2.9. Caribbeans have their principal presence in London and the West Midlands. Indians/African Asians have a higher

presence in the West Midlands than Caribbeans, but this is surpassed in London where approximately one fifth of the population of those wards in which they live are Indians/ African Asians (note that since the Census does not distinguish between Indians and African Asians, the own ethnic group densities for these groups refer to the proportions of Indians and African Asians combined). Pakistanis also appear well-established in the West Midlands, but it is in West Yorkshire where the Pakistani proportion of the wards in which they live is at its highest. For Bangladeshis, the highest presences are in London and Greater Manchester. Lastly, those wards in London and outside the major conurbations where Chinese live, have a very low Chinese presence. Overall, the South Asians have the highest presence, with Caribbeans following some way behind and Chinese with a very low presence. This effect is even more localised within London since, as noted before, Indians and African Asians live in different parts of London from those in which Bangladeshis live, so wards in which both Indians/African Asians and Bangladeshis live are few in number.

It is also informative to explore variations in density by type of city. The distinction between London and other cities has already been noted as has that between the inner and outer cities. Since we have also seen evidence that the relationship between the inner city and the surrounding metropolitan area is different in London compared with other cities, Table 2.10 distinguishes between four city types in order to allow us to focus on these differences. Considering the provincial cities, Caribbeans, Indians and Pakistanis in the inner city all live in wards with a higher density than those in the

Table 2.9: Own ethnic group density by conurbation (%)

Conurbation	Ethnic group				
	Caribbean	Indian/African Asian	Pakistani	Bangladeshi	Chinese
London	12	19	5	19	1
Greater Manchester	–	4	10	20	–
South Yorkshire	–	–	10	–	–
West Midlands	10	13	18	4	–
West Yorkshire	8	–	28	–	–
Elsewhere	2	7	11	3	0
All areas	9	13	13	13	1

outer city. Such uniformity is not evident in London, however. Caribbeans in inner London live in wards with a substantially lower minority density than those in outer London. For Indians, there is no difference between inner and outer London. Indians and, in particular, Bangladeshis in inner London, live in areas of high ethnic minority density. For these two ethnic groups, inner London has similar levels of density to other inner city areas. However, for the other main ethnic groups in the inner London (Caribbeans and Chinese) the levels of density are much lower. For all ethnic groups, the levels of density in outer London are higher than those of the metropolitan areas surrounding other city centres.

Table 2.11 shows variations in the representation of individuals' own ethnic groups by type of city. Caribbeans can be seen to have their principal presence in London and other city centres. Indians/African Asians have their highest presence in outer London. Bangladeshis have a high presence in inner London, the highest of any minority ethnic group in any area. Chinese, on the other hand, do not have a substantial presence in any area. Pakistanis are most established outside London, in both the inner and outer city areas.

The concentration of minority ethnic groups

In this section, we refine our consideration of settlement patterns. We have seen already that the major conurbations have higher levels of ethnic minority density than other areas and that there is important variation in density between conurbations. Merely by virtue of living in one of the major conurbations, an individual is likely to live in an area with a higher ethnic minority presence than would be the case outside the major conurbations. However, location within a city is also important since there will typically be a wide variation in ethnic minority density.

Table 2.10: Minority ethnic group density by type of city (%)

Type of city	Ethnic group						
	White	Caribbean	Indian	African Asian	Pakistani	Bangladeshi	Chinese
Inner London	21	29	38	–	–	42	26
Outer London	12	36	39	35	35	–	18
Other inner city	4	39	40	–	43	–	–
Other outer city	3	24	18	17	28	–	–
All cities	8	33	31	32	34	39	22

Table 2.11: Own ethnic group density by type of city (%)

Type of city	Ethnic group				
	Caribbean	Indian/African Asian	Pakistani	Bangladeshi	Chinese
Inner London	13	11	-	24	1
Outer London	12	21	5	-	1
Other inner city	12	12	19	-	-
Other outer city	4	10	18	-	-
All cities	11	16	15	15	1

We can therefore distinguish between differences in minority density *between* cities and *within* cities. This leads us to introduce a conceptual distinction which will recur throughout the analysis. This distinction is between *strategic* reasons for residential location and *tactical* reasons. The strategic reasons dictate the part of the country in which an individual lives. We hypothesise that, since each of the main conurbations can be regarded as self-contained and are beyond daily travelling distance of each other, that there are strategic reasons for being in London rather than Greater Manchester, for example. The main strategic reason for living in a given conurbation is likely to be historical. As already noted, different minority groups had different characteristics in terms of education and qualifications and there were therefore systematic differences in the overall match of ethnic group to job. Given the geographic specialisation of industry in England, the matching of jobs to skills resulted in different ethnic minority groups being more represented in some areas than others. Through serial migration these communities were reinforced and strengthened over time.

The conurbations in which minority ethnic groups are overwhelmingly concentrated differ both in terms of the proportion of the population who are from an ethnic minority and the levels of deprivation. However, within each conurbation, the area in which individuals live is likely to reflect the current preferences and circumstances of that person. These are the tactical reasons for living in a particular area and might include the availability of housing, convenience of transport to work, proximity to family and friends, and so on. For example, a newly affluent ethnic minority family may wish

to remain within a conurbation because of family and community ties, but can afford to live in a less deprived area within that conurbation. Strategic reasons are important in explaining why an individual from an ethnic minority lives in a particular conurbation while tactical reasons are important in explaining why an individual lives in a particular area within that conurbation. Since the tactical decisions are linked to personal preferences and circumstances, we are well placed, through the use of the Fourth Survey, to examine the relationship between ethnic minority density and deprivation on the one hand, and socioeconomic characteristics on the other.

We have operationalised this distinction by expressing ethnic minority density of a ward *relative* to the density of the conurbation. In other words, concentration is calculated as the difference between ward and conurbation ethnic minority density. This allows us to focus solely on the tactical residential decision and to ignore strategic reasons. Some support for abstracting from the strategic reasons in this way is provided by Champion (1996) who showed inter-regional migration to be lower for ethnic minorities as a whole than for whites, but intra-regional migration to be higher than for whites.

Table 2.12 considers a crude division between whites and non-whites and shows clear evidence of minority concentration. Whites in all conurbations live in wards where the density of minority ethnic groups is below the ambient density, with the exception of those living outside the main conurbations who live in wards where the density is, on the whole, the same as the ambient density. There are quite wide variations between conurbations. For example, minority concentration in the 'white' wards of the West Midlands is much lower than in the white wards in London. This is indicative of a lower level of segregation of ethnic minorities in London than the West Midlands. This finding is supported by Peach (1996) who shows the index of dissimilarity (a widely used measure of segregation) between whites and non-whites to be much lower in London than in Birmingham. For ethnic minorities, the reverse is true. In all conurbations, they live in wards where the density of minority ethnic groups is above the ambient density. The highest concentration is found in West Yorkshire.

We can also examine how this varies across ethnic groups. Table 2.13 shows Bangladeshis and Pakistanis to live in wards with the highest concentration. Earlier we showed Bangladeshis to live in wards with the highest minority

density. Once account is taken of minority density at the level of the conurbation, the difference between Bangladeshis and Pakistanis is removed. The ranking of the other ethnic groups is unchanged. There are some inter-conurbation differences. Considering the two major ethnic minority conurbations of London and the West Midlands, we see that concentration is higher in the West Midlands for Caribbeans, Pakistanis and Bangladeshis, but lower for Indians. For African Asians, the difference is more marginal. Pakistanis in West Yorkshire live in wards with the highest concentration of any ethnic minority group in any conurbation.

There is therefore evidence of differences in concentration across ethnic minority groups and between conurbations. Another aspect which is of interest is specialisation – the extent to which particular minorities have established themselves in particular wards. This can be expressed as the ratio of the density of a particular ethnic group to the density of all minority ethnic groups. This will vary between zero and one. A value of zero indicates that the particular ethnic group is not represented at all among the minority ethnic groups in the ward, while a value of one indicates that the particular ethnic group is the only ethnic minority group present in the ward. Consideration of specialisation is clearly relevant when considering the existence or otherwise of ghettos, since we have already noted that one of the defining characteristics of a ghetto is the predominance of a single ethnic minority group.

Table 2.12: Minority ethnic group concentration by conurbation

Conurbation	All ethnic minorities	
	White	Minority
London	-2.6	+13.6
Greater Manchester	-0.2	+10.5
South Yorkshire	-1.6	+15.7
West Midlands	-7.0	+18.9
West Yorkshire	-5.2	+25.0
Elsewhere	0.0	+7.6
All areas	-1.0	+13.1

Table 2.13: Minority ethnic group concentration by conurbation

Conurbation	Ethnic group						
	White	Caribbean	Indian	African Asian	Pakistani	Bangladeshi	Chinese
London	-2.6	+12.0	+18.7	+14.7	+15.9	+19.0	1.0
Greater Manchester	-0.2	-	-	-	+14.3	+27.7	-
South Yorkshire	-	-	-	-	+12.0	-	-
West Midlands	-7.0	+24.2	+10.4	+17.1	+28.5	+28.1	-
West Yorkshire	-5.2	+18.5	-	-	+34.9	-	-
Elsewhere	0.0	+4.8	+8.4	+10.9	+13.7	+13.4	1.8
All areas	-1.0	+12.5	+12.7	+13.1	+19.2	+19.9	3.6

Table 2.14: Minority ethnic group specialisation by conurbation (%)

Conurbation	Ethnic group				
	Caribbean	Indian/African Asian	Pakistani	Bangladeshi	Chinese
London	38	49	11	38	6
Greater Manchester	-	51	43	57	-
South Yorkshire	-	-	73	-	-
West Midlands	30	57	42	07	-
West Yorkshire	27	-	60	-	-
Elsewhere	38	45	60	11	12
All areas	36	49	48	29	9

Table 2.14 shows that specialisation is greatest for Indians/African Asians and Pakistanis. They tend to live in wards where their own ethnic group accounts for approximately half of all minority ethnic groups. Caribbeans have a lower level of specialisation and Bangladeshis lower still. This is a slightly surprising result given the earlier findings on Bangladeshi concentration. Finally, Chinese are shown to have the lowest level of specialisation.

Again there is variation between conurbations. Caribbeans are most specialised in London, Indians/African Asians in the West Midlands, Bangladeshis in Greater Manchester and Pakistanis in South and West Yorkshire. There are high levels of specialisation for all ethnic minority groups who do not live in the major conurbations, with the exception of Bangladeshis and Chinese.

Given our earlier results, it is likely that there will be marked differences in specialisation between London and other cities and between inner and outer city areas. This is explored in Table 2.15. Of particular note is the extent to which Indians and African Asians have a high level of specialisation in outer London while Bangladeshis have a high level in inner London. Caribbeans are more specialised in inner than outer London. As regards other cities, we again see the greater specialisation in the outer city areas for Indians and African Asians. Pakistanis also have a high level of specialisation in these metropolitan areas, but also in the city centres. Again, Caribbeans are more specialised in inner cities than in the surrounding metropolitan areas.

Table 2.15: Minority ethnic group specialisation by type of city (%)

Type of city	Ethnic group				
	Caribbean	Indian/African Asian	Pakistani	Bangladeshi	Chinese
Inner London	44	22	-	49	5
Outer London	32	53	13	-	6
Other inner city	34	27	43	-	-
Other outer city	17	60	59	-	-
All cities	36	50	48	29	9

Deprivation

We have seen how ethnic minorities tend to live in certain conurbations, and within conurbations, in certain wards. In this chapter, we examine the level of deprivation in those areas which are home to minorities. To do this, we make use of the DoE's 1991 deprivation index, as outlined earlier. Analogous to the treatment of ethnic minority density in the preceding chapter, a measure of deprivation for a given conurbation is calculated as the average level of deprivation for the wards within that conurbation. The actual deprivation index is the product of a statistical formula and is not as straightforward to interpret as the density of ethnic minorities in the population of an area. However, it allows a ranking of areas in terms of deprivation. The larger the (positive) value of the deprivation index, the greater is the deprivation in that area. Similarly, the more negative the deprivation index, the lower is deprivation. A value of zero indicates a level of deprivation similar to that in the country as a whole.

In Table 3.1 a measure of deprivation has been calculated for all conurbations as the average of the deprivation scores of each ward within that conurbation. Note that, unlike the other tables, this is not restricted to those wards within conurbations which are represented in the Fourth Survey; rather, all wards within conurbations are used to construct a measure of conurbation-level deprivation using DoE information. It is clear that there is substantial variation, with London having the highest level of deprivation and the West Midlands having the second highest level. These are the two major conurbations for ethnic minorities. Areas outside the main conurbations have the lowest levels. There is also variation when considering deprivation sub-indices. As noted in the introduction, both of these sub-indices are calculated as the sum of a sub-set of the indicators which make up the overall index. Summing the two sub-indices gives the overall index. Most notable is the extent to which London has much higher measured housing deprivation than other conurbations. When considering economic deprivation, we see that this is lowest in wards outside the main conurbations.

Table 3.1: Deprivation of the conurbations

Conurbation	Overall deprivation	Housing deprivation	Economic deprivation	Number of wards
London	5.3	2.4	2.9	764
Greater Manchester	-0.5	-2.8	2.3	214
South Yorkshire	1.4	-2.3	3.7	94
West Midlands	2.4	-1.3	3.7	162
West Yorkshire	-1.1	-2.9	1.8	126
Elsewhere	-4.6	-1.3	-3.3	7,241

Table 3.1 uses DoE data simply to show the level of deprivation in the wards comprising each conurbation, drawing no distinction between those areas populated by whites or by ethnic minority groups. In the tables that follow, we revert to using the Fourth Survey to analyse differences between ethnic groups in the extent to which they are to be found in deprived areas.

Proceeding in the same way as when considering density, Table 3.2 shows the extent to which deprivation is higher in the urban areas than elsewhere. This is clearly the case, as indicated by the lower values of the deprivation index for non-urban areas. Also striking is the lower level of deprivation in those wards populated by whites compared with those populated by ethnic minorities. This is true of both urban and non-urban areas. As we shall see, this is a common finding.

Table 3.2: Deprivation of urban versus non-urban areas

Type of area	White	Minority
Urban area	0.0	8.4
Not urban area	-4.6	-1.3
All types of area	-3.2	5.4

Table 3.3 shows that, when considering only the cities, ward deprivation is much higher for whites in London than in other cities. The same is not true of minorities, however. This higher level of deprivation in London for whites has the effect of narrowing the gap between whites and minorities to the extent that both groups in London live in wards with comparable levels of deprivation.

Table 3.3: Deprivation of London versus other cities

Type of area	White	Minority
London	7.0	8.3
Other cities	-3.2	8.6
All cities	0.0	8.4

Table 3.4 considers the divide between inner city and outer city areas. Inner city wards have higher levels of deprivation than those in outer cities. The differentials between whites and ethnic minorities exist in both parts of the city.

Table 3.4: Deprivation of inner city versus outer city areas

Type of area	White	Minority
Inner city	7.4	13.8
Outer city	-5.2	4.8
All cities	0.0	8.4

As with the analysis of density, we consider in Table 3.5 the division between the inner and outer city in London and the other conurbations. We see that the level of ward deprivation for whites and non-whites is broadly similar only in inner London. Elsewhere whites consistently live in less deprived wards than minorities. Both outer London and the metropolitan areas surrounding other cities are characterised by similar levels of deprivation for whites. This is roughly true for minorities also. However, whites in the centres of provincial cities live in wards with a much lower level of deprivation than those in inner London. For minorities this is not the case: the level of deprivation in inner cities outside London is only slightly below that in inner London itself.

Table 3.5: Deprivation by type of city

Type of city	White	Minority
Inner London	13.6	15.3
Outer London	-5.2	3.9
Other inner city	1.5	11.7
Other outer city	-5.2	6.3
All cities	0.0	8.4

These results bear a striking resemblance to those of the previous chapter. That is to say, in most instances, a higher density of ethnic minorities coincides with a higher level of deprivation. Exceptions to this rule are of great interest. For example, minorities in outer London live in areas with a slightly higher level of ethnic minority density than those in inner London, yet their level of deprivation appears much lower.

Table 3.6 presents deprivation for each of the main conurbations. For minority ethnic groups, those living in South Yorkshire appear to occupy the most deprived wards, although this is based on a relatively small number of households. The levels of deprivation in other cities are fairly comparable, although Greater Manchester has a slightly lower level. Those ethnic minority households which are not in the main conurbations are in the least deprived wards.

For whites, the level of deprivation in London is higher than anywhere else. Still, however, this level is lower than that for minority ethnic groups in London. Deprivation in West Yorkshire and Greater Manchester is dramatically lower than that for minorities, and these levels are actually lower than for those whites who live outside the main conurbations.

Individual ethnic groups

So far, the analysis has considered ethnic minorities as a whole. While this is useful in providing an overview of the extent to which deprivation in white areas differs from that in minority areas, it does not permit any insights into the variations across minority ethnic groups. This is clearly of interest since, as Modood et al (1997) show, there are marked differences between minority ethnic groups in their housing arrangements.

Table 3.7 presents variations in deprivation by conurbation. The findings for whites are the same as those presented earlier but are reproduced here for convenience. Overall, Bangladeshis are shown to live in the most deprived wards, followed by Pakistanis and Caribbeans. Indians live in wards with a slightly higher level of deprivation than those in which African Asians and Chinese live. Whites live in wards with the lowest levels of deprivation.

Table 3.6: Deprivation by conurbation

Conurbation	White		Minority	
	Deprivation	N	Deprivation	N
London	7.1	281	8.3	1,367
Greater Manchester	-6.5	76	4.8	99
South Yorkshire	-7.5	26	13.0	87
West Midlands	4.4	111	8.5	528
West Yorkshire	-8.1	261	8.6	168
Elsewhere	-4.1	2,129	-1.1	1,028
All conurbations	-3.2	2,884	5.4	3,277

N= Number of households

For London, there is substantial variation in deprivation across ethnic groups, with Bangladeshis living in the most deprived wards and Caribbeans close behind. Pakistanis and Chinese live in wards with a similar level of deprivation to those lived in by whites, while Indians and African Asians live in less deprived wards. For Caribbeans, the level of deprivation is higher in London than anywhere else, while for Bangladeshis, Greater Manchester has equally high levels and the West Midlands is only slightly lower. The West Midlands has the highest levels of deprivation for Indians, African Asians and Pakistanis. Pakistanis also live in wards with comparable levels of deprivation in South and West Yorkshire. All minority ethnic groups experience the lowest level of deprivation when living outside the main conurbations. In Greater Manchester and West Yorkshire the deprivation of ethnic minorities relative to whites is very polarised.

Deprivation sub-indices

Table 3.8 shows how housing deprivation varies across ethnic groups and conurbations. The ranking of different ethnic groups is different from that given by the analysis of the full index. It is now Caribbeans who appear the most deprived, marginally ahead of Bangladeshis. There is little difference in the measured housing deprivation of the wards inhabited by the other minority ethnic groups. Whites are still to be found in wards with the lowest levels of housing deprivation.

Table 3.7: Deprivation by ethnic group

| Conurbation | Ethnic group | | | | | | |
	White	Caribbean	Indian	African Asian	Pakistani	Bangladeshi	Chinese
London	7.1	12.2	4.0	1.6	7.8	13.0	6.8
Greater Manchester	-6.5	-	-	-	7.3	12.9	-
South Yorkshire	-	-	-	-	10.4	-	-
West Midlands	4.4	9.0	6.6	8.4	11.5	11.4	-
West Yorkshire	-8.1	7.8	-	-	10.9	-	-
Elsewhere	-4.2	-1.0	-2.7	-1.6	4.8	2.5	-5.5
All conurbations	-3.2	7.9	2.6	1.2	8.0	10.3	1.0

Of those minority ethnic groups living in London, Caribbeans now live in the most deprived wards by this housing definition, with Bangladeshis in second place. Apart from this switching, the ranking of the other ethnic groups has remained largely unchanged. Again, London is the most deprived conurbation for Caribbeans and Bangladeshis, but now this is by a wide margin. Pakistanis in London now appear more deprived relative to other ethnic groups than when considering the 'full' deprivation index. This difference between London and the other conurbations has increased for all minority ethnic groups indicating the extent of housing deprivation in the capital. In fact, by this measure, London has the highest level of deprivation for all minority ethnic groups. This distinction is not as marked for white households.

Table 3.9 shows that the ordering of ethnic groups by the economic sub-index is again different from that indicated by the full index. While Bangladeshis are shown to be most deprived, it is now Pakistanis who are in second place. Caribbeans live in the next most economically deprived wards, followed by Indians, African Asians and, finally, Chinese. Whites continue to live in the least deprived wards, according to this definition.

In London, Bangladeshis live in the most economically deprived wards, followed by Caribbeans. Pakistanis and Chinese have quite a similar level of deprivation which is slightly higher than that of whites. Indians and, in particular, African Asians appear to live in wards with the lowest level of economic deprivation. Deprivation is higher in Greater Manchester than London for Pakistanis and, in particular, Bangladeshis who have their highest level of economic deprivation in this conurbation. For other South Asians, it is in the West Midlands where this form of deprivation is highest. This level of deprivation for Pakistanis is matched in West Yorkshire. Their lowest level of economic deprivation is shown to be in London. For whites, Greater Manchester and West Yorkshire appear to offer the lowest levels of economic deprivation.

Table 3.8: Deprivation by ethnic group: housing sub-index

| Conurbation | Ethnic group | | | | | | |
	White	Caribbean	Indian	African Asian	Pakistani	Bangladeshi	Chinese
London	3.4	4.3	1.9	0.9	3.1	4.0	2.7
Greater Manchester	-1.9	-	-	-	-1.4	-0.7	-
South Yorkshire	-	-	-	-	0.0	-	-
West Midlands	0.4	0.4	-0.8	-0.6	-0.3	0.7	-
West Yorkshire	-4.0	0.7	-	-	-0.4	-	-
Elsewhere	-1.8	-1.4	-1.4	-1.3	-0.8	-1.1	-2.0
All conurbations	-1.4	2.0	-0.1	-0.2	0.1	1.8	0.3

Table 3.9: Deprivation by ethnic group: economic sub-index

Conurbation	Ethnic group						
	White	Caribbean	Indian	African Asian	Pakistani	Bangladeshi	Chinese
London	3.6	7.9	2.1	0.7	4.8	9.1	4.1
Greater Manchester	-4.6	–	–	–	8.6	13.6	–
South Yorkshire	–	–	–	–	10.4	–	–
West Midlands	4.0	8.5	7.5	9.0	11.7	10.7	–
West Yorkshire	-4.1	7.2	–	–	11.3	–	–
Elsewhere	-2.4	0.4	-1.3	-0.3	5.7	3.6	-3.5
All conurbations	-1.8	6.0	2.7	1.3	8.0	8.5	0.8

There appears to be a demarcation between London and the other conurbations. In the capital, deprivation is principally related to housing. In other conurbations, it is the economic aspects of deprivation which are more important.

However, there is an important proviso to this finding. As discussed in the introduction, the housing deprivation sub-indices are based on just two indicators: 'children in unsuitable accommodation' and 'households lacking amenities'. These are both rather unsatisfactory. Consistent national small-area data that effectively capture the different housing circumstances of households simply do not exist. Percentages of 'households lacking amenities' are now at very low national levels, except for certain private-rented tenures, and this means that small variations can have disproportionate statistical effects. To a lesser extent, the same is true of 'children in unsuitable accommodation' since this largely reflects the incidence of flats. (The results from the updated [1996] and revised deprivation index are due to be published in 1998. The 'children in unsuitable accommodation' indicator is dropped from the index.) The Census does not enable one to identify the quality of these flats. Since high-status flats are relatively common in certain London boroughs, the level of deprivation in these boroughs is therefore likely to be overstated. Hence, the difference in housing deprivation between London and the other conurbations is likely to be less marked than that shown in Table 3.8.

Relative deprivation

It is not just the level of deprivation which is of interest. As mentioned earlier, a key focus of this study is the extent to which minority ethnic groups are to be found disproportionately within deprived wards. Thus, assuming once again that households are more likely to move within than between conurbations, a principal concern is the extent to which minorities locate in wards with a level of deprivation that is high relative to that of the conurbation. In order to examine this, deprivation for each of the conurbations was calculated as the average level of deprivation across the wards in that conurbation. The index of *relative* deprivation is then calculated as the difference between ward deprivation and conurbation deprivation. Clearly, a positive value indicates a higher level of deprivation in the ward than in the conurbation as a whole, and a negative value indicates a lower level. (Note that the DoE's deprivation index is itself a relative index, comparing all areas to a national level of zero. The 'relativity' in this analysis is a local rather than a national one.)

Table 3.10 shows the effect of considering relative rather than absolute deprivation. Comparing these figures to those in Table 3.6 highlights a number of differences. For example, although in absolute terms ethnic minorities in London live in wards with a level of deprivation similar to that in the West Midlands and West Yorkshire, in relative terms, these wards are less deprived than those in any other conurbation. This is a consequence of the high level of deprivation in London, as reported in Table 3.1. The same is true, to a lesser extent, of those in the West Midlands.

The effect on individual ethnic groups is shown in Table 3.11. The rankings within each conurbation are unchanged from those presented in Table 3.7 since the same measure of conurbation deprivation has been deducted from the level of deprivation for each ethnic group in that conurbation. It is the differences between conurbations which are of more interest. Across all conurbations, Pakistanis and Bangladeshis are the ethnic groups living in the wards with the highest degree of deprivation relative to that of their conurbation. Caribbeans now follow some way behind. Indians and Chinese have a lower level of relative deprivation, while whites and African Asians have the lowest level of all.

By a similar rationale, we can examine the extent to which aspects of ward deprivation vary from that of the conurbation. In Table 3.12 we consider the housing deprivation index discussed earlier. As with the full index, this is now reformulated as the difference between ward and conurbation housing deprivation. The main difference when considering relative housing deprivation is that London no longer stands out as it did in Table 3.8. Once the high ambient level of housing deprivation is taken into account, housing deprivation in London appears more in line with that in other conurbations. The pattern within conurbations

Table 3.10: Relative deprivation by conurbation

Conurbation	White		Minority	
	Deprivation	N	Deprivation	N
London	+1.8	281	+3.0	1,367
Greater Manchester	-6.0	76	+5.3	99
South Yorkshire	-9.0	26	+11.7	87
West Midlands	+2.0	111	+6.1	528
West Yorkshire	-7.0	261	+9.7	168
Elsewhere	+0.5	2,129	+3.5	1,028
All conurbations	-0.3	2,884	+4.3	3,277

N= Number of households

is unchanged from that in Table 3.8. Taking all conurbations as a whole, Caribbeans, Bangladeshis and Pakistanis have the highest levels of relative housing deprivation.

Since economic deprivation is more evenly spread across conurbations, the change when considering relative rather than absolute deprivation is not so dramatic. The most striking change shown in Table 3.13 is for those in wards outside the main conurbations for whom relative deprivation is higher than the absolute deprivation presented in Table 3.9. For example, all South Asians in London are less relatively deprived than those outside the main conurbations. Finally, taking all conurbations as a whole, Pakistanis and Bangladeshis appear to have the highest level of relative economic deprivation followed by Caribbeans.

Table 3.11: Relative deprivation by ethnic group

Conurbation				Ethnic group			
	White	Caribbean	Indian	African Asian	Pakistani	Bangladeshi	Chinese
London	+1.7	+6.9	-1.4	-3.7	+2.5	+7.7	+1.5
Greater Manchester	-6.0	-	-	-	+7.8	+13.4	-
South Yorkshire	-	-	-	-	+9.0	-	-
West Midlands	+2.0	+6.6	+4.3	+6.0	+9.1	+9.0	-
West Yorkshire	-7.0	+8.9	-	-	+12.0	-	-
Elsewhere	+0.5	+3.6	+1.9	+3.0	+9.4	+7.1	-0.9
All conurbations	-0.3	+6.2	+1.5	-0.2	+8.3	+8.4	+1.4

Table 3.12: Relative housing deprivation by ethnic group

Conurbation	Ethnic group						
	White	Caribbean	Indian	African Asian	Pakistani	Bangladeshi	Chinese
London	+1.0	+1.9	-0.6	-1.5	+0.7	+1.5	+0.2
Greater Manchester	+0.9	-	-	-	+1.4	+2.1	-
South Yorkshire	-	-	-	-	+2.3	-	-
West Midlands	+1.7	+1.7	+0.5	+0.7	+1.0	+2.0	-
West Yorkshire	-1.2	+3.5	-	-	+2.5	-	-
Elsewhere	-0.5	0.0	-0.1	+0.1	+0.5	+0.2	-0.7
All conurbations	-0.3	+1.5	+0.0	-0.6	+1.2	+1.4	+0.4

Table 3.13: Relative economic deprivation by ethnic group

Conurbation	Ethnic group						
	White	Caribbean	Indian	African Asian	Pakistani	Bangladeshi	Chinese
London	+0.8	+5.0	-0.8	-2.2	+1.9	+6.2	+1.2
Greater Manchester	-6.9	-	-	-	+6.3	+11.3	-
South Yorkshire	-	-	-	-	+6.7	-	-
West Midlands	+0.3	+4.9	+3.8	+5.3	+8.1	+7.0	-
West Yorkshire	-5.9	+5.4	-	-	+9.5	-	-
Elsewhere	+0.9	+3.6	+2.0	+3.0	+8.9	+6.9	-0.2
All conurbations	0.0	+4.7	+1.5	+0.5	+7.2	+7.0	+1.0

The relationship between ethnic minority density and deprivation

In this section, we consider the relationship between ethnic minority density and deprivation. We have suggested already that areas where ethnic minorities live tend to be deprived. Here we examine in a little more depth the nature of that relationship.

In Figure 3.1 we consider this relationship at the level of the conurbation. These measures of density and deprivation relate to the conurbation as a whole and are not limited to the Fourth Survey sample. What is striking is that there appears to be a linear relationship between density and deprivation (a line showing this has been added to the graph); the only outliers to this relationship being the conurbations of South Yorkshire and, to a lesser extent, Greater Manchester. These two outliers account for only a small proportion of all ethnic minorities, so for the majority of our sample, there appears to be a straightforward relationship: the more deprived a city is, the more minority group members live there.

Figure 3.1: The relationship between ethnic minority density and deprivation at the conurbation level

In Figure 3.2, the relationship between ward minority density and deprivation for each ethnic group is examined. In order to better visualise the relationships, a smoothed line was fitted which comes close to representing the relationship in each case. These suggest that for all ethnic groups, areas of high deprivation tend to have high densities of minority residents. However, there are substantial differences between ethnic groups. In particular, the curve is flattest for whites, indicating that, for them, a rise in ward level deprivation is associated with only a small rise in ethnic minority density. This finding was borne out by regression analysis that showed the slope of the curve to be smaller for whites than for any ethnic minority group (the slope was steepest for Indians). Another feature for many of the ethnic minority groups was that at low levels of deprivation the curve is quite flat but that, after a certain point, it becomes much steeper. This suggests that there may be only a weak link between density and deprivation in those less deprived wards, but that this relationship becomes stronger as deprivation rises.

Figure 3.2: Ward level density and deprivation, by ethnic group

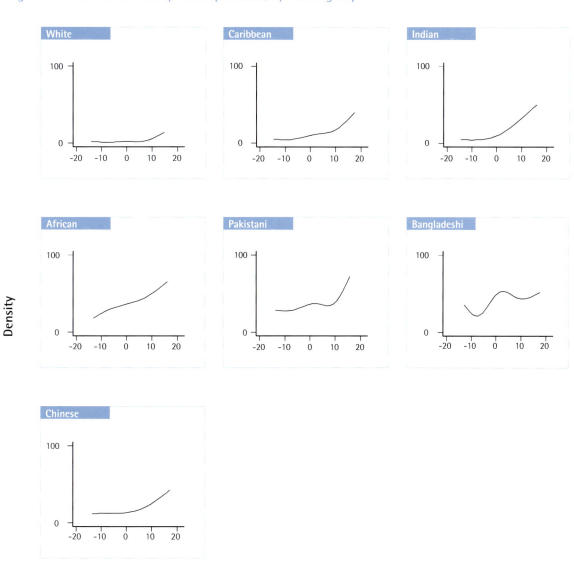

Density

Deprivation

Given our earlier arguments, we are also interested in *relative* measures of minority density (ie, concentration) and deprivation. Figure 3.3 follows a similar form to Figure 3.2. Again the fitted lines suggest a difference between whites and ethnic minorities, namely, that the relationship between concentration and relative deprivation is not very marked for those wards in which whites live. Furthermore, there is again evidence that the relationship may be non-linear. This is supported by the results of regression analysis. The strength of the association between the two factors was substantially reduced when we considered *relative* measures (compared with the simple analysis in Figure 3.2). Thus, part of the explanation for the association lies in the fact that London and the West Midlands, where most minorities live, are also highly deprived. But it remains true that within London, the West

Midlands and other cities, the minorities tend to be found in less well-off neighbourhoods.

These findings are important since they indicate that wards with high levels of ethnic minority density also have high levels of deprivation. While earlier sections have indicated that ethnic minorities tend to live in wards with a high minority density and also that they tend to live in wards which are deprived, this section has drawn these separate results together to provide support for the assertion that areas with a high ethnic minority density tend also to have a high level of deprivation. However, this relationship is far from being an exact one: there are some deprived wards which are occupied almost entirely by white people; and some areas with many minority residents which are not deprived. And, as the graphs show, these relationships are stronger for some groups than for others.

Figure 3.3: Ward level concentration and relative deprivation, by ethnic group

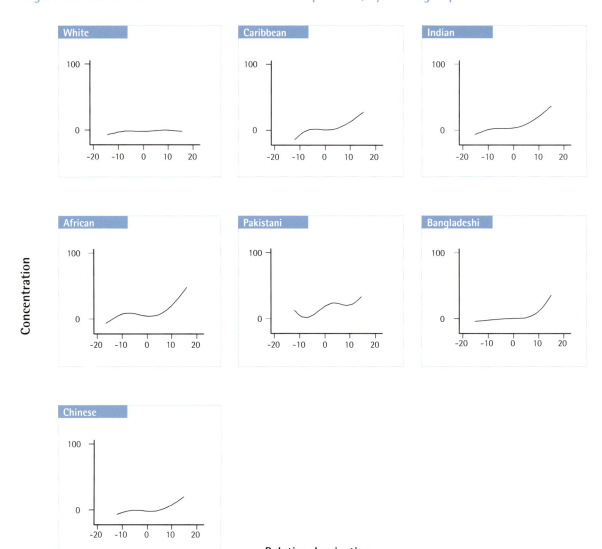

Relative deprivation

4

The effect of personal characteristics

In this chapter, we examine the extent to which personal and household characteristics influence whether an individual lives in a ward with high concentration or relative deprivation. As in the previous two chapters, these relative measures are calculated as the difference between ward and conurbation measures of density and deprivation, and therefore ignore inter-conurbation influences. There is no distinction at this stage between different ethnic minority groups since at this level of disaggregation many cells in the tables would become too small to permit general trends to be identified. This is deferred until the next chapter when we examine relative deprivation and concentration using a statistical model.

Each of the tables that follow shows how individuals with a particular attribute, or living in a household characterised by a particular attribute, tend to live in wards with a high level of deprivation or ethnic minority concentration. Our earlier discussion might lead us to expect similar patterns to be revealed by the two indicators. However, this is not always so.

We begin by considering ethnic minorities only. In Table 4.1 there does not appear to be any consistent pattern in relative deprivation by years since migration. However, with the exception of those who migrated more than 35 years ago, there is some tendency for more recent migrants to live in wards with a high ethnic minority concentration. This provides some evidence of dispersal over time, although this trend is not marked. Those born in the UK live in wards with the lowest concentration. By contrast they are more likely than most others to live in areas of high relative deprivation.

Table 4.1: Relative deprivation and concentration by years since migration

Years since migration	Relative deprivation	Concentration
Less than 5 years	+4.6	+16.5
5 to 14 years	+4.7	+14.1
15 to 24 years	+2.4	+14.0
25 to 34 years	+4.5	+12.5
35 or more years	+5.2	+13.8
Born in the UK	+5.1	+12.2
All	+4.3	+13.1

It is interesting to consider the extent to which relative deprivation and concentration are associated with cultural attributes. An index to capture the strength of ethnic identity was calculated for a sub-sample of the South Asians only. This index combines three culture specific attributes (language, clothes and religion) into one overall measure. Dividing the scores on this index into quartiles resulted in four categories of behavioural identity (Modood et al, 1997). For our analysis, the labels for these quartiles range from 'very high' to 'very low'. Table 4.2 shows that those with a 'very low' score on the behavioural identity index stand out as living in wards with lower level of deprivation and concentration than other South Asians. In terms of deprivation, this appears closely linked with strength of ethnic identity.

Table 4.2: Relative deprivation and concentration by index of behavioural identity (South Asians only)

Behavioural identity index	Relative deprivation	Concentration
Very low	-0.7	+8.3
Low	+2.9	+19.4
High	+3.7	+16.3
Very high	+6.0	+17.4
All	+2.8	+15.2

The results by religion are also striking. Table 4.3 shows that among South Asians, Muslims tend to live in wards with a high level of relative deprivation and a high minority ethnic concentration. Hindus and Sikhs, on the other hand, live in wards with quite high concentration but a low level of deprivation. This is interesting since it provides an example of the divergence of relative deprivation and concentration and indicates the possibility of some relatively well-off ethnic minority communities. It suggests that some ethnic minority groups may *choose* to live in an area of high ethnic minority concentration rather than living in such an area as an inevitable consequence of living in a deprived area.

Table 4.3: Relative deprivation and concentration by religion (South Asians only)

Religion	Relative deprivation	Concentration
None	+1.1	+8.4
Hindu	+0.1	+13.9
Sikh	+1.7	+12.8
Muslim	+7.9	+19.7
Christian	-1.5	+2.9
Other	-2.4	+10.0
All	+3.3	+15.0

Respondents for whom religion is a very important part of life live in more deprived wards than those with no religion or for whom religion is not important. This result is not altogether surprising since it is among Muslims that the highest proportion (three quarters) describe religion as being very important to

them. They also tend to live in wards with a higher ethnic minority concentration, although this effect is not so marked. This is shown in Table 4.4.

Table 4.4 Relative deprivation and concentration by importance of religion (South Asians only)

Importance of religion	Relative deprivation	Concentration
No religion/not important	+0.7	+13.8
Very important	+5.4	+17.3
All	+3.3	+15.7

We now return to considering all ethnic groups rather than just South Asians. Table 4.5 below considers the ethnic mix of partnership. Individuals in all-white partnerships live in wards with the lowest level of relative deprivation. Those in all-Bangladeshi and all-Pakistani partnerships live in wards with the highest level of deprivation. The salient point is that where there is a mixed family type with a white member plus a minority ethnic member, the level of deprivation is very low, comparable to that of all white partnerships.

In terms of concentration, we see again the result that while those in all-Indian partnerships may live in areas of low deprivation, they also live in areas of high concentration. This suggests the possibility of communities of relatively affluent Indians. Individuals in all-white partnerships live in wards with the lowest levels of concentration, followed by those in mixed white/minority partnerships.

Table 4.5: Relative deprivation and concentration by ethnic mix of partnership

Ethnic mix	Relative deprivation	Concentration
All white	-0.3	-1.0
All Caribbean	+7.0	+14.0
All Indian	+1.2	+14.1
All Pakistani	+8.6	+19.4
All Bangladeshi	+8.9	+21.2
All Chinese	+2.4	+4.0
White/minority	+0.2	+2.6

In the remaining tables we consider both whites and ethnic minorities. Table 4.6 shows that for whites there is little evidence of any relationship between age and deprivation, although their level of deprivation is lowest for those in the 35 to 64 age group. For minorities, it is among the oldest and the youngest that both relative deprivation and concentration are at their highest.

Table 4.6: Relative deprivation and concentration by age

Age	Whites	Minorities	
	Relative deprivation	Relative deprivation	Concentration
16 to 24 years	+0.2	+6.4	+16.1
25 to 34 years	+0.3	+4.1	+12.1
35 to 64 years	–1.0	+3.7	+12.5
65 plus years	+0.2	+6.3	+17.2
All	–0.3	+4.3	+13.1

Table 4.7 shows that being partnered is associated with living in a ward with lower deprivation. This is true for both whites and ethnic minorities. Lone parents live in wards with the highest level of deprivation. The same pattern is evident when considering concentration, although not nearly so marked.

Table 4.7: Relative deprivation and concentration by family type

Family type	Whites	Minorities	
	Relative deprivation	Relative deprivation	Concentration
Partnered, no children	–0.9	+3.0	+12.3
Partnered, children	–1.3	+3.2	+12.7
Single, no children	+0.5	+6.3	+14.2
Single, children	+2.4	+7.1	+14.3
All	–0.3	+4.3	+13.1

We can also examine how relative deprivation and concentration vary with the individual's level of qualification. Table 4.8 shows that, for whites, those who are more qualified live in wards with a lower level of deprivation. The 'other' category is broadly defined and therefore difficult to interpret. For minorities there is a stronger pattern – the higher the level of educational achievement, the lower is deprivation. The same overall pattern is evident when considering concentration, but now it is less clearly defined: those whose highest qualification is a CSE live in areas with a lower concentration than those who have 'O'-levels or equivalent.

Table 4.8: Relative deprivation and concentration by qualification

Highest qualification	Whites	Minorities	
	Relative deprivation	Relative deprivation	Concentration
None	+0.6	+7.0	+17.4
Other	+1.1	+4.1	+10.6
CSE (not grade1)	+0.0	+6.7	+13.4
'O'-level or equivalent	–1.4	+4.4	+15.6
'A'-level or equivalent	–0.9	+2.2	+10.5
Degree	–1.1	–0.2	+7.6
All	–0.3	+4.3	+13.1

Table 4.9 shows that the more paid workers there are in a household, the lower the level of deprivation. This is true for both whites and minorities, although it is interesting to note that for whites the difference between those households where all adults are unemployed and those where all adults are retired is much more marked than for ethnic minorities. For ethnic minorities, concentration varies in a similar way; those individuals in households with no workers live in wards with a higher concentration, and this falls as the number of workers increases. Interestingly, it jumps for those households with three or more workers.

Table 4.9: Relative deprivation and concentration by employment status

Employment status	Whites	Minorities	
	Relative deprivation	Relative deprivation	Concentration
No workers in household	+1.0	+7.4	+16.4
One worker in household	-0.7	+4.3	+13.2
Two workers in household	-1.3	+1.6	+10.0
Three or more workers in household	-1.3	+1.5	+11.2
No workers in household because			
All adults unemployed	+3.2	+7.8	+16.5
All adults retired	+0.4	+6.4	+14.0

The next two tables consider standard of living as proxied by income and consumer durables. Table 4.10 shows that households with a higher level of equivalent income (total income adjusted to take account of household size) are more likely to be in wards with a low level of deprivation and ethnic minority concentration. It is only among ethnic minority households in the two lowest income classifications that this trend is disturbed, with those having equivalent income of £45 to £60 per week living in wards with a higher deprivation and concentration than those with an equivalent income of less than £45 per week

Table 4.10: Relative deprivation and concentration by household equivalent income

Household equivalent income	Whites	Minorities	
	Relative deprivation	Relative deprivation	Concentration
Less than £45	+4.6	+8.1	+16.5
£45-£60	+2.1	+8.5	+17.9
£60-£80	+1.7	+6.4	+15.0
£80-£100	+1.2	+6.4	+15.1
£100-£145	-0.2	+3.5	+12.8
£145-£200	-0.7	+3.3	+11.9
£200-£300	-1.7	+0.9	+7.8
More than £300	-2.4	-0.6	+4.2
Don't know/refused	-1.3	+3.1	+14.0
All	-0.3	+4.3	+13.1

This highlights the distinction between area-level deprivation and household-level disadvantage. Both whites and ethnic minorities tend to live in more deprived areas, the lower their income. We might imagine that minorities live in more deprived areas than whites just because of their income. However, as Table 4.10 shows, minorities live in areas which are more deprived than their income would lead us to expect. This points to a specific effect of belonging to an ethnic minority (although we shall see that this is not true of all ethnic minorities in all conurbations).

A clear trend is also apparent when considering the number of consumer durables. For whites, there is a strong negative relationship between the number of household durables and the level of deprivation. This is shown in Table 4.11. Those ethnic minority households with more consumer durables are likely to be situated in wards with a relatively low level of deprivation. This is also true when considering ethnic minority concentration. Now, however, although there is an overall reduction in concentration as the number of consumer durables increases, there is no difference between those households having three to four consumer durables and those having five to six.

Table 4.11: Relative deprivation and concentration by number of household consumer durables

Number of consumer durables	Whites	Minorities	
	Relative deprivation	Relative deprivation	Concentration
0-2	+3.8	+9.7	+21.3
3-4	+1.3	+8.1	+17.4
5-6	+1.0	+6.5	+17.4
7-8	-0.2	+3.9	+11.6
9-11	-2.4	-0.5	+6.7
All	-0.3	+4.3	+13.1

Table 4.12 shows that those whites who own or are buying property which was previously privately owned live in less deprived wards than those with other types of tenure. This is also true for minority ethnic groups although now the difference between those in social accommodation and those who have bought or are buying from social housing are much more

marked. Pakistanis are likely to prove a notable exception to this since they are characterised by high levels of both home ownership and poverty (Modood et al, 1997). Those ethnic minorities who are in social or shared accommodation live in the most deprived areas. In terms of concentration, ethnic minorities who rent privately are in the wards with the highest concentration, while those who have bought from social housing are in wards with the lowest concentration.

Table 4.12: Relative deprivation and concentration by tenure type

| Tenure type | Whites | Minorities | |
	Relative deprivation	Relative deprivation	Concentration
Owned/buying from private	-2.2	+2.2	+12.8
Owned/buying from social housing	+2.6	+5.7	+10.5
Social or shared accommodation	+2.9	+8.2	+13.7
Private rented	+1.5	+6.0	+16.1
Other	-	-	-
All	-0.3	+4.3	+13.1

Table 4.13 considers the number of basic household amenities which are either absent or shared. These amenities include a fixed bath or shower, a bathroom, a kitchen, an inside flush toilet, a telephone and a garden, yard or patio. Those whites who have exclusive use of all these basic amenities live in wards with the least deprivation and the lowest concentration and there is a clear relationship between the number of basic amenities which are shared or absent and the level of relative deprivation. The pattern for ethnic minorities, however, is not as expected. Those who lack sole use of two or more amenities appear to live in less deprived areas than those who lack sole use of only one. In addition, those lacking sole use of two or more amenities appear to live in wards with a lower concentration than those who lack sole use of only one. Why this should be so is not obvious.

Table 4.13: Relative deprivation and concentration by number of basic amenities shared/absent

| Number of basic amenities shared/absent | Whites | Minorities | |
	Relative deprivation	Relative deprivation	Concentration
Exclusive use of all	-0.7	+3.4	+12.0
One shared/absent	+1.7	+8.1	+17.4
Two or more	+2.5	+6.6	+16.9
All	-0.3	+4.3	+13.1

Considering overcrowding, there is a clearer pattern. Table 4.14 shows that minority households with more persons per room tend to live in more deprived areas. The difference is particularly marked between the two highest categories. Similarly, with concentration, those households which are more crowded tend to be in wards with a higher level of concentration. However, the differences across the three categories are more evenly spread than when considering relative deprivation which jumps sharply in the highest category.

Table 4.14: Relative deprivation and concentration by number of persons per room

| Persons per room | Whites | Minorities | |
	Relative deprivation	Relative deprivation	Concentration
Fewer than 0.5	-0.5	+3.9	+11.2
0.5 to 0.99	+0.2	+4.1	+14.1
1 or more	-	+8.0	+17.9
All	-0.3	+4.3	+13.1

5

Modelling relative deprivation and concentration

The preceding tabular analysis has shown some interesting results. In this chapter, those characteristics which are associated with relative deprivation and concentration are examined more formally within the framework of a statistical model. This provides two major benefits. First, it allows us to assess the extent to which our findings are statistically significant. Second, it allows consideration of more than one relationship at a time. With the tabular analysis, we are constrained as to how many variables can be considered at once. It is possible, through the construction of ever more complicated tables, to gain some insight into the interaction between key variables. However, the estimation of a statistical model allows us to achieve this result much more completely and transparently.

The modelling approach and the estimation results are given in Appendix B. In this chapter we examine the effects of individual and household characteristics on relative deprivation and concentration by showing the predicted levels of relative deprivation and concentration for a number of differently defined individuals.

Relative deprivation

In Table 5.1 we consider the predicted relative deprivation of the wards in which a 'reference' individual would live. This reference individual is defined (arbitrarily) as not being an owner-occupier, being fluent in English and in social class IIIn (Registrar General definition). S/he lives in London in a household which has seven to eight consumer durable goods and a weekly equivalent income of £100. In addition, the

white individuals are assumed to be 45 years old and to live in centrally heated accommodation (these additional assumptions for white individuals are required since age and central heating were found to be significant in modelling concentration and relative deprivation, whereas for ethnic minorities, these variables were insignificant).

We can see that there is considerable variation across ethnic groups in the level of relative deprivation of the wards in which they live. We note first that whites tend to live in wards with a higher level of relative deprivation than Indian and African Asian Hindus. This is similar to the finding in Table 3.11, although the differences are now less marked. Pakistanis and Chinese tend to live in wards with equal levels of relative deprivation. Bangladeshis and, in particular, Caribbeans are shown to live in the most deprived wards.

We can also see the effect of having a higher or a lower equivalent income. In the second row of Table 5.1 the typical levels of deprivation are shown for individuals who are identical to the reference case except that they have a weekly equivalent income of £50 rather than £100. This has a similar effect across all ethnic groups; reducing the level of income leads to an increase in the typical level of relative deprivation. By contrast, an increase in income will reduce the typical level of deprivation, as shown in the third row. This result is eminently plausible, but it is interesting that, for ethnic minorities, the strength of this relationship diminishes as income increases, to the extent that, for those at the top of the income distribution, no such relationship exists.

Table 5.1: Relative deprivation: the effect of income

				Ethnic group			
	White	Caribbean	Indian (Hindu)	African Asian (Hindu)	Pakistani	Bangladeshi	Chinese
Reference individual	+2.6	+8.0	+1.9	+0.2	+3.2	+6.6	+3.1
Equivalent income of £50/week	+3.1	+8.7	+2.6	+0.9	+3.9	+7.4	+3.8
Equivalent income of £200/week	+1.8	+6.9	+0.8	-0.9	+2.1	+5.5	+2.0

In Table 5.2, we consider the effect of owner-occupation and social class. We can see that, for all ethnic groups, being an owner-occupier is associated with living in an area with lower relative deprivation than other tenure arrangements. The effect for whites is slightly smaller than that for other ethnic groups with the exception of Pakistanis. This lesser effect for Pakistanis is perhaps explained by the generally low standard of housing which they typically own; Modood et al (1997) show their home ownership to be concentrated in low quality terraced housing.

The effect of social class is as expected: being in a higher social class is associated with lower relative deprivation. The size of this effect is quite consistent across ethnic groups. Being educated to 'A'-level standard or higher does not affect the typical level of relative deprivation for whites. For minorities, however, its effect is more important and it serves to reduce the level of deprivation by the same amount for all minority ethnic groups.

The results set out in Appendix B show that there is significant variation across conurbations in the typical relative deprivation of ethnic groups. The pattern of variation is very complex and difficult to interpret. In Table 5.3 we consider individuals living in the West Midlands, the most important conurbation for ethnic minorities after London. The pattern across ethnic groups is very mixed. Whites now live in the wards with the lowest levels of relative deprivation by a substantial margin, despite their deprivation being slightly higher than in London. For most other ethnic groups, there has been a large increase. This is particularly noticeable for Chinese, although since this is based on only a small number of Chinese in the West Midlands, it should be regarded with some caution. For the other ethnic groups, there are no such qualifications. The increase is particularly large for African Asian and Indian Hindus, whose level of deprivation in the West Midlands is similar to that of Pakistanis. Bangladeshis have the

Table 5.2: Relative deprivation: the effect of owner-occupation, social class and education

				Ethnic group			
	White	Caribbean	Indian (Hindu)	African Asian (Hindu)	Pakistani	Bangladeshi	Chinese
Reference individual	+2.6	+8.0	+1.9	+0.2	+3.2	+6.6	+3.1
Owner-occupier	+0.1	+5.0	-1.1	-2.8	+2.2	+3.7	+0.1
Social class 1	+0.5	+5.9	-0.3	-2.0	+1.0	+4.5	+0.9
Social class 5	+3.1	+9.1	+3.0	+1.2	+4.3	+7.7	+4.2
Educated to 'A'-level standard or higher	+2.6	+6.2	+0.0	-1.7	+1.3	+4.8	+1.2

Table 5.3: Relative deprivation: the effect of living in the West Midlands

| | Ethnic group | | | | | | |
	White	Caribbean	Indian (Hindu)	African Asian (Hindu)	Pakistani	Bangladeshi	Chinese
Reference individual	+2.6	+8.0	+1.9	+0.2	+3.2	+6.6	+3.1
Lives in the West Midlands	+3.0	+7.1	+7.6	+7.6	+7.5	+9.4	+12.4

highest level of relative deprivation. Interestingly, for Caribbeans, the level of relative deprivation is lower in the West Midlands than for London. They are the only ethnic group for which this is true.

In the preceding tables we have considered only Indians and African Asians who were Hindus. In Table 5.4 we see how relative deprivation varies with religion among these ethnic groups for the reference individual. Sikhs can be seen to live in wards with a slightly lower level of relative deprivation, although this difference is more marked for African Asians. Conversely, Muslims live in wards with a higher level of deprivation. This is particularly true for Indian Muslims, who live in wards with a much higher level of deprivation than Indian Hindus or Sikhs.

Table 5.4: Relative deprivation: the effect of religion (Indians and African Asians only)

| | Ethnic group | |
	Indian	African Asian
Hindu	+1.9	+0.2
Sikh	+1.2	-1.6
Muslim	+5.2	+1.7

Concentration

In Table 5.5 we consider concentration. The reference individual is likely to live in a ward with a much lower ethnic minority density than London as a whole if s/he is white or Chinese. That whites live in wards with a low concentration is evidence of their segregation

from other ethnic groups. The low levels of concentration for Chinese in London has been noted elsewhere (Peach, 1996) and is possibly explained by their strong links to restaurants. There is also a noticeable South Asian effect. Indian and African Asian Hindus, Pakistanis and Bangladeshis all live in wards with high levels of concentration. It is interesting to compare this with Table 2.13 which shows Bangladeshis to live in wards with the highest levels of concentration. When we control for other variables, we see that out of all South Asians, Bangladeshis tend to live in wards with the lowest minority concentration. This is a reflection of the fact that, in reality, Bangladeshis have the lowest levels of fluency in English and live in households with the smallest number of consumer durables of all ethnic groups. By assuming fluency and the presence of more consumer durables than exist in the Bangladeshi population, their typical level of concentration falls accordingly. Caribbeans live in wards with a level of concentration below that of the South Asians.

We can also see from Table 5.5 the effect of income. For whites, this effect is almost non-existent. It appears that their level of income has no effect on whether they live in an area with higher concentration. For the minority ethnic groups, there is an effect. Specifically, those on lower incomes will tend to live in areas with higher concentration and vice versa.

In Table 5.6, we see that owner-occupation increases concentration for all ethnic groups, although the effect is only slight (and, in fact, insignificant) for whites. In terms of social class, we see that those in the highest social class live in areas with a lower concentration. This effect is more marked for whites than for

Table 5.5: Concentration: the effect of income

			Ethnic group				
	White	Caribbean	Indian (Hindu)	African Asian (Hindu)	Pakistani	Bangladeshi	Chinese
Reference individual	-3.4	+10.0	+18.0	+14.3	+17.4	+13.0	-3.0
Equivalent income of £50/week	-3.4	+10.7	+18.6	+15.0	+18.1	+13.7	-2.3
Equivalent income of £200/week	-3.3	+8.6	+16.6	+12.9	+16.0	+11.6	-4.3

other ethnic groups, with the exception of Indian and African Asian Hindus in the highest social classes for whom the difference is even more pronounced. Conversely, those in the lowest social group are likely to live in wards with a higher level of concentration. The size of this effect is uniform across ethnic minorities and is much greater than the effect for whites.

Similarly, while being educated to at least 'A'-level has little effect on concentration for whites, those ethnic minorities with qualifications at this level are likely to live in wards with a lower level of concentration, once other factors are accounted for. By contrast, those who are not fluent in English are more likely to live in areas with a higher ethnic minority concentration. Pakistanis appear to provide an interesting exception to this: for them, being fluent in English is associated with

living in an area with a lower level of concentration.

The effect of living in the West Midlands rather than London is considered in Table 5.7. The effect varies quite markedly across ethnic groups. For whites, living in the West Midlands is associated with living in wards with a lower level of ethnic minority concentration than in London. For Caribbeans, the reverse is true – they are likely to live in wards with a much higher level of concentration. Considering the South Asians, the effect is more mixed. Pakistanis and, especially, Bangladeshis will tend to live in wards with a higher level of concentration in the West Midlands than in London. For Indian and African Asian Hindus, living in the West Midlands is associated with living in wards with a lower concentration. This effect is particularly marked for Indians.

Table 5.6: Concentration: the effect of owner-occupation, social class, education and fluency in English

			Ethnic group				
	White	Caribbean (Hindu)	Indian (Hindu)	African Asian	Pakistani	Bangladeshi	Chinese
Reference household	-3.4	+10.0	+18.0	+14.3	+17.4	+13.0	-3.0
Owner-occupier	-3.0	+13.4	+21.3	+17.7	+20.8	+16.4	+0.4
Social class 1	-5.3	+9.3	+13.2	+10.6	+16.6	+12.2	-3.7
Social class 5	-2.4	+16.0	+23.9	+20.2	+23.3	+18.9	+3.0
Educated to 'A'-level standard or higher	-3.6	+8.9	+16.8	+13.1	+16.3	+11.8	-4.1
Not fluent in English		+12.2	+20.1	+16.4	+15.6	+15.2	-0.8

Table 5.7: Concentration: the effect of living in the West Midlands

	Ethnic group						
	White	Caribbean	Indian (Hindu)	African Asian (Hindu)	Pakistani	Bangladeshi	Chinese
Reference household	-3.4	+10.0	+18.0	+14.3	+17.4	+13.0	-3.0
Lives in the West Midlands	-8.0	+19.2	+7.0	+11.7	+19.4	+22.1	+18.1

Finally, we note the association between religion and the concentration of those wards in which Indians and African Asians live. Table 5.8 shows that there is not a consistency across religions. For Indians, Muslims are the most likely to live in areas of high concentration, and Sikhs will live in areas with the lowest concentration. For African Asians, however, it is the Hindus who live in the areas of highest ethnic minority concentration. For all three religions, the associated level of concentration is higher for Indians than for African Asians.

Table 5.8: Concentration: the effect of religion (Indians and African Asians only)

	Ethnic group	
	Indian	African Asian
Hindu	+18.0	+14.3
Sikh	+16.2	+10.9
Muslim	+21.7	+12.7

Discussion

Armed with these results, we are in a position to address two of the fundamental questions which have been implicit throughout this analysis.

To what extent do ethnic minorities tend to live in areas which are more deprived or concentrated than the areas of residence of white people?

We have seen already that the answer to this question is complex and subject to geographical variation. Restricting our attention to the two principal conurbations for ethnic minorities, we see that South Asians in London, with the exception of Bangladeshis, live in wards with a level of deprivation which is similar to that of whites and substantially below that of Caribbeans. This is after controlling for personal and household characteristics. In the West Midlands, the divide between whites and non-whites is much greater but there is less difference between the minority groups. In particular, South Asians live in wards with, if anything, a slightly higher level of deprivation than Caribbeans. We might have expected a similar pattern to be evident when we consider ethnic minority concentration, but this is not so. While whites in both conurbations live in wards with much lower levels of concentration than those in which minorities reside, the evidence suggests a tendency among South Asians to live in wards with a high concentration regardless of their level of deprivation.

Thus, whites appears to live in areas of low ethnic minority concentration regardless of their level of deprivation. This is shown most powerfully in the case of London where, despite having levels of deprivation similar to those of some ethnic minorities, they always have levels of concentration much lower than other ethnic groups. Another important point arising from this analysis is the extent to which there is a South Asian 'effect' in London with this non-dispersing group tending to build communities in wards of relative affluence.

How are individual/household characteristics associated with relative deprivation and concentration?

The relationship between circumstances and deprivation is as expected: those individual characteristics which are commonly associated with a lower standard of living are also associated with deprivation. Concentration is more interesting. Many of the same associations with individual characteristics are found as when considering deprivation. For example, lower income, fewer consumer durables, being in lower social classes and being less qualified were all factors which served to increase the likelihood of living in a ward with a higher ethnic minority concentration. However, there were some important differences. Fluency in English was significantly associated with living in a ward with a higher ethnic minority concentration (although strangely not for Pakistanis). This makes intuitive sense since those not fluent in English may prefer to live in areas where their own language is represented, while, at the same time, where a non-English-speaking community exists, this may reduce the incentive for an individual to acquire fluency in English.

A major difference was also found when tenure was considered. Whereas owner-occupation has been shown to have a negative association with deprivation, the reverse is true when considering ethnic minority concentration. That is to say, an owner-occupier from an ethnic minority is more likely to live in an area with high minority concentration than is someone with an alternative tenure arrangement (except privately renting which is shown to have a similar effect to owner-occupation). Taking these two findings together suggests the possibility of a 'community' of relatively affluent ethnic minority owner-occupiers, after controlling for other factors.

6 Conclusions and implications

It is clearly important to urban policy to understand more fully the spatial distribution of ethnic minorities and, in particular, their over-representation in deprived areas. Given this over-representation, a key question for urban policy is the extent to which regeneration programmes are meeting the needs of ethnic minorities. There is some recognition in national policy of the need to address issues specific to ethnic minorities. For example, procedures under the Single Regeneration Budget have improved the requirement for ethnic monitoring (Chelliah, 1995).

A number of programmes include projects which are run by and for ethnic minority communities. Nevertheless, the overall conclusion of the few studies and analyses of this issue (Chelliah, 1995; Crook, 1995; Hausner and associates, 1992; Medas, 1993) is that both the process and the out-turn have been disappointing. Ethnic minority communities have not been adequately involved in the planning and implementation of programmes; their employment and housing prospects have not been improved.

The conclusion of general evaluations of the urban programme may not be much more optimistic (Robson et al, 1994), but we are struck by an important contradiction in much of the mainstream writing about regeneration policy (Fordham, 1995; Taylor, 1995). On the one hand, great importance is placed on involving the residents in the development and management of regeneration activities while, on the other hand, there has been a virtual absence of any direct reference to ethnic minorities in this involvement. The DoE's substantial handbook on consultation was typical in containing just two incidental references to minority groups (DoE, 1995). The implication seems to be that ethnic minorities are not expected to have a point of view distinct from that of their white neighbours. However, more recently there has been some redress; the newest guidance from the DETR on involving communities in urban regeneration includes a chapter on involving ethnic minorities (DETR, 1997).

Another striking point to emerge from existing research and analysis is that ethnic minorities are seen to form a single group. This is true of both mainstream work and reports taking a specific ethnic minority perspective. In the 1980s it was common to label all minority groups 'black' as a way of emphasising their common experience in a racist society (Smith, 1989; Modood, 1994). They may share that, but recent research has emphasised the wide variations between minority groups in their household structures, their economic positions, their cultural perspectives and so on (Jones, 1993; Modood et al, 1997). A single policy will not work if one group needs creches for lone parents, another needs investment capital for small businesses and a third needs lessons in English.

It is widely acknowledged that benefits do not automatically 'trickle down' from infrastructural improvements to the people in greatest need, or from prestige projects to the residents in nearby areas. By the same token, attempts to consult or to meet the needs of all the people of an area do not necessarily reach each minority group. Regeneration programmes have often adopted what is known as a 'colour-blind' approach (Ben-Tovin, 1987). In this, as in other fields, general improvements in policy may be desirable, but they do not reduce racial disadvantage as a by-product. There have, however, been a number of local initiatives where multicultural consultative structures have been developed (Rex and Samad, 1996).

This research was intended to enable regeneration policy to focus more sharply on ethnic issues. To facilitate this, we have explicitly considered the extent to which different ethnic groups live in areas of high deprivation and/or ethnic minority density. The results have vindicated the separate treatment of different minority ethnic groups since we have seen significant variations between minorities in the extent to which they live in areas of high deprivation and minority density. Furthermore, the analysis has gone further than this. By including socioeconomic characteristics, we control for factors which vary between ethnic groups but are related to deprivation and concentration. In this way, the effects of ethnicity, after taking account of other factors, can be identified.

It is perhaps useful to consider the proportion of each ethnic group living in wards with a high level of relative deprivation or concentration. Table 6.1 considers those wards whose level of relative deprivation or ethnic minority concentration places them in the top 10% of all wards represented in our sample. (The wards included in the sample are not a cross-section of all wards – they are biased towards high concentration.) We can then see the proportion of each ethnic group living in a ward with a high level of relative deprivation or concentration by this definition. To capture the most extreme wards, we also consider the top 5%. If there were no variations between ethnic groups, the expected proportions would be 10% and 5% respectively, for each ethnic group. The results are quite striking. Nearly a quarter of Bangladeshis live in the most relatively deprived wards on the 10% definition, and one tenth on the 5% definition. Pakistanis are not far behind. Caribbeans are not as prevalent in the top 10% of deprived wards, but the proportion in the top 5% is high. Whites, Indians and African Asians display similar patterns. In terms of concentration, Bangladeshis again stand out, particularly when considering the 5% definition. Only among Indians and African Asians are the proportions for concentration higher than for

deprivation; this provides further support for the existence of relatively well-off communities among these ethnic groups.

Table 6.1: Percentage of each ethnic group living in wards with high relative deprivation or concentration

	Deprivation		Concentration	
	Top 10%	*Top 5%*	*Top 10%*	*Top 5%*
White	5	4	1	1
Caribbean	12	8	10	5
Indian	6	3	12	7
African Asian	5	4	11	4
Pakistani	21	7	19	7
Bangladeshi	23	11	23	17
Chinese	11	5	1	1

Throughout the analysis, a distinction has been drawn between simple measures of deprivation and ethnic minority density on the one hand, and measures relative to the conurbation on the other. Both are important. Simple measures are an appropriate focus for urban policy since it is these measures which essentially define the problem facing those involved in the regeneration process or the alleviation of poverty. That is to say, an area has a level of deprivation which exists irrespective of the level of deprivation in the local conurbation. However, relative measures also provide useful information since, by focusing on those individuals living in wards which have high levels of deprivation relative to the ambient deprivation level, we are able to identify those characteristics that increase the risk of an individual living in a deprived area. Another interpretation of the relevance of these two definitions of deprivation and density is that the simple measure is more relevant to policy at the national level while the relative measure is more applicable to policy at the local level.

There is a further complexity in the analysis. We have seen throughout that the relative deprivation and ethnic minority concentration of a ward are related characteristics. However, when trying to understand the policy implications of high ward deprivation compared to the policy implications of high ward ethnic minority density, different issues are relevant. It is fairly innocuous to assume that most individuals would, if they had free choice, opt to live in a ward which did not have a high level of deprivation. Thus, if we were only concerned with deprivation, the analysis in this report could be useful in identifying target groups to improve the areal aspects of their standard of living. However, considering ethnic minority density is not as straightforward. We cannot assume that most ethnic minorities would wish to live in an area of low minority density. In fact, the reverse is more likely to be the case (Modood et al, 1997). This makes the issue of policy implications less straightforward than when considering deprivation. The intractability of the issue is further compounded when one considers that preferences on the ethnic minority density of the wards in which minorities live are likely to be shaped, at least in part, by racist influences in wider society. Again, we see that both choices and constraints have a role to play in determining whether an individual lives in a ward with high minority density. All this produces an ambiguity when considering the policy implications of living in wards with a high ethnic minority density.

The research has allowed a fuller understanding of the patterns of settlement for ethnic minority groups. We have abstracted from the historic reasons for settling in particular conurbations and have mainly focused on the types of wards within each conurbation in which ethnic minorities live. This seems appropriate given the migration patterns for minority ethnic groups within Britain. Champion (1996) showed inter-regional migration to be lower for ethnic minorities as a whole than for whites, but intra-regional migration to be higher than for whites. For both deprivation and density we have shown considerable variations both between and within ethnic groups. This also accords with Champion's analysis which shows that Caribbeans, for example, have a very high propensity for intra-regional migration while Indians and Pakistanis have a much lower propensity; lower, in fact, than whites.

Unsurprisingly, deprivation at ward level among ethnic minorities is shown to be correlated with those individual characteristics which are commonly associated with a lower standard of living. Those with lower incomes, fewer consumer durables, in lower social classes, who did not own their accommodation and who

were less qualified were more likely to live in wards with a higher level of deprivation. This was also broadly true of whites, with the proviso that some characteristics were not statistically significant and others, such as age, became significant. When we considered ethnic minority concentration many of the same associations with individual characteristics were found as when considering deprivation although, as we have seen, there were also a number of important differences.

After controlling for these individual and household characteristics, there were still clear effects associated with ethnicity. This is a powerful result since, in effect, it states that there is something about different ethnic groups which predisposes them, to differing degrees, to living in areas of high deprivation and high concentration. However, the observed tendency to live in deprived wards may have a number of explanations. It may be that there is some characteristic which is related to deprivation but on which information is not collected in the Fourth Survey. However, it is not immediately obvious what such a characteristic might be since the Survey attempted to collect enough information to ascertain standard of living. If, on the other hand, we accept that the variables included in the model adequately capture the economic strength of individuals, and thus their ability to choose between types of ward in which to live, the inference is that belonging to an ethnic minority group increases the risk of living in more deprived wards for reasons that are non-economic in nature. There are two obvious possibilities. The first is that ethnic minorities may be limited in the extent to which they can move into areas with lower deprivation. In other words, discrimination may operate so as to prevent the free movement of ethnic minorities to wards having a level of deprivation which reflects their financial standing. The second is that ethnic minorities may wish to live in an area where other ethnic minorities and/or their own ethnic group are well-represented; living in a ward with a high level of deprivation is the price that must be paid to fulfil this wish. Kempson (1998), in her study of Bangladeshi households in Tower Hamlets, shows that families were prone to turn down the offer of improved accommodation if it meant moving away from the Bangladeshi community. This was prompted both by the desire to maintain their social network and by safety considerations.

However, there is some evidence of certain ethnic minority communities existing in wards of relative affluence yet high minority concentration. This is particularly true of South Asians in London, with the exception of Bangladeshis. There is some variation between religions with Indian and African Asian Muslims standing out as being associated with higher deprivation. Storkey and Lewis (1997) show there to be quite marked divides between the Indian and African Asian areas of London: Ealing and Hounslow has a largely Punjabi Sikh population, Harrow and Brent is an area of settlement for many African Asians of Gujerati origin while in Newham and Redbridge Sikhs, Hindus and Muslims are all well-represented.

It is among South Asians that the levels of minority density and specialisation reach their highest levels. Concentration in the US, on the other hand, is associated primarily with African-Americans. In both the US and the UK, concentration and deprivation are associated with the inner city. However, for South Asians (excluding Bangladeshis), their main area of concentration is in outer London. Here they not only live in areas with a high minority presence, they also represent a substantial proportion of the population. Indians and African Asians in outer London make up more than half of the minority population. In this regard, there appears to be a parallel with France where the outer city *banlieues* are the areas of highest ethnic minority population. However, whereas in France the *banlieues* are also associated with high deprivation, this is not the case in outer London. Thus, in the case of South Asians, the generalisation that concentration is synonymous with deprivation is broken. This provides a strong suggestion that such South Asian enclaves exist, at least in part, as a result of voluntaristic attraction rather than negatively imposed constraints.

This is an interesting result and suggests that South Asian patterns of settlement may be better explained by a pluralist rather than an assimilationist model. This is in line with the findings of Peach (1997) who shows that South Asian patterns of settlement in London are better described by the pluralist model, while Caribbean patterns are more assimilationist. That is to say that for South Asians, economic progress is not inevitably tied to geographic dispersal; distinct ethnic enclaves are maintained during upward movement in socioeconomic class.

In terms of additional comparisons with the US situation, there is clearly no equivalent to the African-American ghettos. It is interesting to question why Caribbeans, as the UK group most similar to African-Americans, have a level of concentration so much lower than that of the South Asians. Is this a reflection of a difference between Caribbeans and African-Americans, or is it a reflection of a difference between society in the UK and society in the US? The answer to this question is not obvious but it is important to bear in mind that in the UK the experience of immigration is much more recent than in the US where African-Americans have lived for generations.

Thus, the US model of segregation is not applicable to the UK; no ethnic minority group can be said to be truly 'ghettoised'. Instead, a different model is necessary to understand patterns of ethnic minority settlement in the UK. Such a model must acknowledge the differences between ethnic groups – South Asians, for example, are typically non-dispersing to a greater degree than Caribbeans – while allowing a role for individual characteristics. As the ethnic minority population matures, these individual characteristics may become increasingly important as determining factors. The contribution of this report is in highlighting the variation between minority ethnic groups and identifying how personal and household characteristics impact on where ethnic minorities live.

References

Ben-Tovin, G. (1987) 'Race, local politics and urban regeneration strategy – Lessons from Liverpool', in B. Foley (ed) *Regenerating the cities*, Manchester: Manchester University Press.

Champion, T. (1996) 'Internal migration and ethnicity in Britain', in P. Ratcliffe (ed) *Social geography and ethnicity in Britain: Geographical spread, spatial concentration and internal migration*, vol 3 of *Ethnicity in the 1991 Census*, London: HMSO.

Chelliah, R. (1995) *Race and regeneration: A consultative document*, London: Local Government Information Unit.

Crook, J. (1995) *Invisible partners: The impact of the SRB on black communities*, Black Training and Enterprise Group.

DETR (Department of the Environment, Transport and the Regions) (1997) *Involving communities in urban and rural regeneration*, London: HMSO.

DoE (Department of the Environment) (1995) *Involving communities in urban and rural regeneration: A guide for practitioners,* London: HMSO.

Duncan, O. and Duncan, B. (1957) *The negro population of Chicago*, Chicago: University of Chicago Press.

Fordham, G. (1995) *Made to last: Creating sustainable neighbourhood and estate regeneration*, York: Joseph Rowntree Foundation.

Hausner, V. and associates (1992) *Economic revitalisation of inner cities: The Urban Programme and ethnic minorities*, London: HMSO.

Jones, T. (1993) *Britain's ethnic minorities*, London: PSI.

Kempson, E. (1998) *Overcrowding among Bangladeshi households in Tower Hamlets*, London: PSI.

Massey, D. and Denton, N. (1993) *American Apartheid*, Yale: Harvard University Press.

Medas, M. (1993) *From City Challenge to the Single Regeneration Budget: A black perspective*, Sia.

Modood, T. (1994) 'Political blackness and British Asians', *Sociology*, vol 28, no 4.

Modood, T., Berthoud, R., Lakey, J., Nazroo, J., Smith, P., Virdee, S. and Beishon, S. (1997) *Ethnic minorities in Britain*, London: PSI.

OPCS (Office of Population Censuses and Surveys) (1996) *Ethnicity in the 1991 Census*, London: HMSO.

Peach, C. (1996) 'Does Britain have ghettos?', *Transactions of the Institute of British Geographers*, vol 21, no 1.

Peach, C. (1997) 'Pluralist and assimilationist models of ethnic minority settlement in London 1991', *Tijdschrift voor economische en sociale geografie*, vol 88, no 2.

Rex, J. and Samad, Y. (1996) 'Multiculturalism and political integration in Birmingham and Bradford', *Innovation*, vol 9, no 1.

Robson, B. et al (1994) *Assessing the impact of urban policy*, London: HMSO.

Robson, B. and Tye, R. (1995) 'A matrix of deprivation in English Authorities', in *1991 Deprivation Index: A review of approaches and a matrix of results,* London: HMSO.

Smith, P. (1989) *The politics of 'race' and residence,* Cambridge: Polity Press.

Smith, P. and Prior, G. (1996) *The Fourth National Survey of Ethnic Minorities: Technical report*, London: SCPR.

Storkey, M. and Lewis (1997) *Capital divided*, London: London Research Centre.

Taylor, M. (1995) *Unleashing the potential: Bringing residents to the centre of regeneration*, York: Joseph Rowntree Foundation.

Appendix A:
A note on the limitations of the data

Since we are interested not only in minority ethnic groups as a whole but also individually, we must examine separate ethnic groups. This gives rise at times to a practical problem of having too few observations. It is not always possible to retain adequate cell size as shown in the table below. For some cells, the numbers of respondents is too small to allow confidence in the results. Clearly, the results for Chinese will be the least reliable, but also results for all ethnic groups in South Yorkshire will be dubious as will a number of results for Greater Manchester and West Yorkshire. To provide some (albeit arbitrary) safeguard against unreliable findings, those results based on fewer than 30 households are not presented.

Number of households in the Fourth Survey by ethnic group and conurbation

Type of area	Ethnic group							
	White	All minorities	Caribbean	Indian	African Asian	Pakistani	Bangladeshi	Chinese
London	274	1334	484	274	214	126	178	57
Greater Manchester	80	148	6	15	26	63	36	2
South Yorkshire	26	60	11	3	–	39	1	6
West Midlands	113	676	196	223	44	160	46	7
West Yorkshire	263	209	43	22	14	121	5	4
Elsewhere	2130	831	204	198	132	180	51	66
All areas	2886	3258	994	735	430	689	317	142

Appendix B:
Modelling approach

Two equations were estimated in order to examine the extent to which individual characteristics are related to the relative deprivation and the ethnic minority concentration of the wards in which individuals live. Relative deprivation and concentration are significantly correlated such that if an individual is in a ward with a high level of relative deprivation, this ward is also likely to have a high ethnic minority concentration. In view of this correlation, the two equations were modelled jointly using an approach known as Seemingly Unrelated Regression Estimation (SURE). This approach is appropriate when the error term (ie, that variation in the dependent variable – relative deprivation or concentration – which is left unexplained by the explanatory variables) of one equation is correlated with that of another. Statistical tests emphatically showed this to be the case. Exploiting this correlation allows us to improve the efficiency of our estimates.

Two models were estimated – one for ethnic minorities and one for whites. It would have been possible to estimate the model separately for each ethnic group. However, through the inclusion of appropriate explanatory variables, it is possible to estimate a single model for ethnic minorities which gives results equivalent to those which would be provided by estimating separate models for each ethnic group. Estimating just one equation for all ethnic

minority groups has the advantage that those personal characteristics which do not vary across ethnic groups in their effect on relative deprivation and concentration can be identified and treated as having a common effect. This allows us to focus more precisely on those characteristics which do vary in their effect across minority ethnic groups. It also helps with the problem of small sample size for some ethnic groups. The reference ethnic group was arbitrarily chosen as Caribbeans. In theory, it would be possible to estimate just one model which included white households as well. In practice, however, the survey design differed between white and ethnic minority households and does not allow us to estimate a model based on a pooled dataset comprising these two separate samples. For this reason, separate models were estimated for whites and for ethnic minorities.

The design of the Fourth National Survey does not allow the combination of the ethnic minority sample and the white sample into a larger sample representative of all ethnic groups. With the model for whites, as far as possible an equivalent parameter set has been retained in order to permit comparisons to be made between whites and minority ethnic groups. Thus, some socioeconomic characteristics appear in the model despite the fact that they are statistically insignificant in their association with deprivation or concentration.

Model results: ethnic minorities

	Relative deprivation		Concentration	
	Coefficient	P-value	Coefficient	P-value
Constant	11.55	0.00	12.10	0.00
Owner-occupier (y=1,n=0)	-2.99	0.00	3.39	0.00
Pakistani* owner-occupier	2.04	0.00		
Privately renting (y=1,n=0)			4.09	0.00
Equivalent income (£/week)	-0.02	0.00	-0.01	0.00
Square of equivalent income	0.00	0.00		
Income information missing (y=1,n=0)	-2.03	0.00	-2.09	0.00
Number of household durables	-1.01	0.00	-2.24	0.00
Chinese* number of household durables	-1.10	0.00		
Indian* number of household durables			-1.99	0.00
African Asian* number of household durables			-1.92	0.01
Social class I (y=1,n=0)	-2.48	0.00	-0.24	0.87
Social class II (y=1,n=0)	-1.29	0.00	1.20	0.24
Social class IIIn (y=1,n=0)	-0.33	0.42	0.53	0.57
Social class IV (y=1,n=0)	0.47	0.19	3.90	0.00
Social class V (y=1,n=0)	0.74	0.21	6.45	0.00
Social class missing (y=1,n=0)	0.57	0.05	2.35	0.00
Indian* Social class 1 or 2			-3.94	0.00
African Asian* Social class 1 o r2			-2.93	0.05
Educated to 'A'-level or higher (y=1,n=0)	-1.87	0.00	-1.16	0.03
Indian* no religion	1.07	0.25	9.87	0.00
Indian* Hindu	0.54	0.27	14.76	0.00
Indian* Sikh	-0.21	0.62	13.03	0.00
Indian* Muslim	3.84	0.00	18.49	0.00
Indian* Christian	-2.20	0.02	3.28	0.24
Indian* other religion	2.56	0.14	11.59	0.01
African Asian* no religion	-1.97	0.26	3.34	0.47
African Asian* Hindu	0.51	0.36	17.14	0.00
African Asian* Sikh	-1.24	0.07	13.79	0.00
African Asian* Muslim	2.04	0.01	15.56	0.00
African Asian* Christian	0.45	0.77	11.12	0.01
African Asian* other religion	-2.21	0.17	13.31	0.00
Pakistani (y=1,n=0)	3.11	0.00	3.37	0.01
Bangladeshi (y=1,n=0)	2.30	0.00	8.10	0.00
Chinese (y=1,n=0)	0.81	0.50	-1.10	0.39
Fluent in English (y=1,n=0)			-2.18	0.00
Indian* age of youngest child			-0.09	0.00
African Asian* age of youngest child			-0.12	0.00
Pakistani* fluent in English			4.02	0.00
London (y=1,n=0)	1.40	0.00	7.66	0.00
Greater Manchester (y=1,n=0)	4.07	0.00	16.31	0.00
South Yorkshire (y=1,n=0)	8.77	0.00	10.91	0.00
West Midlands (y=1,n=0)	0.48	0.18	16.81	0.00
West Yorkshire (y=1,n=0)	2.69	0.00	8.84	0.00
Indian* London	-6.66	0.00		
African Asian* London	-8.36	0.00	-5.98	0.00
Pakistani* London	-7.95	0.00		
Bangladeshi* London	-3.68	0.00	-5.13	0.05
Chinese* London	-2.43	0.00	-11.88	0.00
Indian* Greater Manchester	-5.61	0.00	-27.20	0.00

	Coefficient	P-value	Coefficient	P-value
African Asian* Greater Manchester	-7.41	0.00	-30.85	0.00
Pakistani* Greater Manchester	-7.09	0.00	-17.94	0.00
Bangladeshi* Greater Manchester			-9.61	0.10
Pakistani* South Yorkshire	-10.10	0.00	-12.77	0.00
Indian* West Midlands			-20.06	0.00
African Asian* West Midlands			-17.67	0.00
Pakistani *West Midlands	-2.73	0.00	-7.17	0.00
Bangladeshi* West Midlands			-5.13	0.13
Chinese* West Midlands	7.79	0.00		
African Asian* West Yorkshire	6.36	0.00		
Pakistani* West Yorkshire			13.79	0.00
Bangladeshi* West Yorkshire			-7.40	0.33

Model results: whites

	Relative deprivation		Concentration	
	Coefficient	P-value	Coefficient	P-value
Constant	8.81	0.00	0.97	0.07
Age	-0.03	0.00		
Central heating (y=1,n=0)	-1.30	0.00		
Owner-occupier (y=1,n=0)	-2.46	0.00	0.35	0.31
Privately renting (y=1,n=0)			0.76	0.18
Equivalent income (£/week)	-0.01	0.00	0.00	0.62
Square of equivalent income	0.00	0.11		
Income information missing (y=1,n=0)	-1.63	0.00	-0.04	0.92
Number of household durables	-0.82	0.00	-0.46	0.00
Social class I (y=1,n=0)	-2.73	0.00	-1.78	0.01
Social class II (y=1,n=0)	-0.97	0.01	0.11	0.78
Social class IIIn (y=1,n=0)	-0.59	0.23	0.15	0.77
Social class IV (y=1,n=0)	0.82	0.10	0.84	0.10
Social class V (y=1,n=0)	-0.15	0.85	1.14	0.15
Social class missing (y=1,n=0)	-0.41	0.26	-0.13	0.73
Educated to 'A'-level or higher (y=1,n=0)	0.00	1.00	-0.24	0.39
London (y=1,n=0)	0.35	0.44	-3.18	0.00
Greater Manchester (y=1,n=0)	-6.39	0.00	-0.35	0.67
South Yorkshire (y=1,n=0)	-9.04	0.00	-1.45	0.28
West Midlands (y=1,n=0)	0.76	0.27	-7.78	0.00
West Yorkshire (y=1,n=0)	-7.71	0.00	-5.18	0.00